C-589   CAREER EXAMINATION SERIES

This is your
PASSBOOK for...

Plasterer

Test Preparation Study Guide
Questions & Answers

NATIONAL LEARNING CORPORATION®

COPYRIGHT NOTICE

This book is SOLELY intended for, is sold ONLY to, and its use is RESTRICTED to individual, bona fide applicants or candidates who qualify by virtue of having seriously filed applications for appropriate license, certificate, professional and/or promotional advancement, higher school matriculation, scholarship, or other legitimate requirements of education and/or governmental authorities.

This book is NOT intended for use, class instruction, tutoring, training, duplication, copying, reprinting, excerption, or adaptation, etc., by:

1) Other publishers
2) Proprietors and/or Instructors of "Coaching" and/or Preparatory Courses
3) Personnel and/or Training Divisions of commercial, industrial, and governmental organizations
4) Schools, colleges, or universities and/or their departments and staffs, including teachers and other personnel
5) Testing Agencies or Bureaus
6) Study groups which seek by the purchase of a single volume to copy and/or duplicate and/or adapt this material for use by the group as a whole without having purchased individual volumes for each of the members of the group
7) Et al.

Such persons would be in violation of appropriate Federal and State statutes.

PROVISION OF LICENSING AGREEMENTS – Recognized educational, commercial, industrial, and governmental institutions and organizations, and others legitimately engaged in educational pursuits, including training, testing, and measurement activities, may address request for a licensing agreement to the copyright owners, who will determine whether, and under what conditions, including fees and charges, the materials in this book may be used them. In other words, a licensing facility exists for the legitimate use of the material in this book on other than an individual basis. However, it is asseverated and affirmed here that the material in this book CANNOT be used without the receipt of the express permission of such a licensing agreement from the Publishers. Inquiries re licensing should be addressed to the company, attention rights and permissions department.

All rights reserved, including the right of reproduction in whole or in part, in any form or by any means, electronic or mechanical, including photocopying, recording, or by any information storage and retrieval system, without permission in writing from the Publisher.

Copyright © 2024 by
National Learning Corporation

212 Michael Drive, Syosset, NY 11791
(516) 921-8888 • www.passbooks.com
E-mail: info@passbooks.com

PUBLISHED IN THE UNITED STATES OF AMERICA

PASSBOOK® SERIES

THE *PASSBOOK® SERIES* has been created to prepare applicants and candidates for the ultimate academic battlefield – the examination room.

At some time in our lives, each and every one of us may be required to take an examination – for validation, matriculation, admission, qualification, registration, certification, or licensure.

Based on the assumption that every applicant or candidate has met the basic formal educational standards, has taken the required number of courses, and read the necessary texts, the *PASSBOOK® SERIES* furnishes the one special preparation which may assure passing with confidence, instead of failing with insecurity. Examination questions – together with answers – are furnished as the basic vehicle for study so that the mysteries of the examination and its compounding difficulties may be eliminated or diminished by a sure method.

This book is meant to help you pass your examination provided that you qualify and are serious in your objective.

The entire field is reviewed through the huge store of content information which is succinctly presented through a provocative and challenging approach – the question-and-answer method.

A climate of success is established by furnishing the correct answers at the end of each test.

You soon learn to recognize types of questions, forms of questions, and patterns of questioning. You may even begin to anticipate expected outcomes.

You perceive that many questions are repeated or adapted so that you can gain acute insights, which may enable you to score many sure points.

You learn how to confront new questions, or types of questions, and to attack them confidently and work out the correct answers.

You note objectives and emphases, and recognize pitfalls and dangers, so that you may make positive educational adjustments.

Moreover, you are kept fully informed in relation to new concepts, methods, practices, and directions in the field.

You discover that you are actually taking the examination all the time: you are preparing for the examination by "taking" an examination, not by reading extraneous and/or supererogatory textbooks.

In short, this PASSBOOK®, used directedly, should be an important factor in helping you to pass your test.

PLASTERER

DUTIES AND RESPONSIBILITIES
Under direction, prepares plastering materials and applies same to interior and exterior surfaces. Performs related work.

EXAMPLES OF TYPICAL TASKS
Prepares or directs the preparation of plastering materials common to the trade such as lime putty, gypsum mortar, Keene cement, etc. Works with plastering materials in the application of scratch, brown and finish coats to interior and exterior surfaces such as walls, ceilings, piers, columns, etc. Does ornamental and cove plastering for new or alteration work as directed. Sets up, checks and works from platforms and scaffolds, depending upon job requirements. Reads and follows plans and specifications. May supervise assigned personnel. Keeps job and other records.

TESTS
The multiple-choice test is designed to assess the extent to which candidates have certain abilities determined to be important to the performance of the tasks of a Plasterer. Task areas to be tested are as follows: work preparation and layout; plastering; tiling; the use of tools, knowledge of plastering materials, application of plaster, defects in plastering, reading comprehension, reporting and record keeping; work site safety; and supervision of staff.

The test may also include questions requiring the use of any of the following abilities:
Written Comprehension: understanding written sentences and paragraphs. Example: A Plasterer might use this ability when reviewing written work orders.
Written Expression: using English words or sentences in writing so that others will understand. Example: A Plasterer might use this ability when describing work completed.
Number Facility: adding, subtracting, multiplying and dividing quickly and correctly. Example: A Plasterer might use this ability when determining the length and width of a wall in order to lay tiles.
Information Ordering: correctly following a rule or set of rules or actions in a certain order. The rule or set of rules must be given. The things or actions to be put in order can include numbers, letters, words, pictures, procedures, sentences, and mathematical or logical operations.
Example: A Plasterer might use this ability when following specific procedures when repairing or replacing a damaged wall.
Problem Sensitivity: being able to tell when something is wrong or likely to go wrong. Example: A Plasterer might use this ability when assigned to repair or replace part of a wall and sees that the entire wall must be replaced.
Manual Dexterity: being able to make skillful coordinated movements of one hand, a hand together with its arm, or two hands to grasp, place, move or assemble objects, such as hand tools or blocks. Example: A Plasterer might use this ability when assigned to mix plaster or apply plaster to a wall.

Certain questions may need to be answered on the basis of documents or other information supplied to the candidates on the date of the multiple-choice exam.

There will also be a qualifying practical test that will assess the candidate's ability to prepare plastering materials and apply such materials to interior and exterior surfaces. Only those candidates who pass the multiple-choice test and meet the education and experience requirements will be scheduled to take the practical test.

HOW TO TAKE A TEST

I. YOU MUST PASS AN EXAMINATION

A. WHAT EVERY CANDIDATE SHOULD KNOW

Examination applicants often ask us for help in preparing for the written test. What can I study in advance? What kinds of questions will be asked? How will the test be given? How will the papers be graded?

As an applicant for a civil service examination, you may be wondering about some of these things. Our purpose here is to suggest effective methods of advance study and to describe civil service examinations.

Your chances for success on this examination can be increased if you know how to prepare. Those "pre-examination jitters" can be reduced if you know what to expect. You can even experience an adventure in good citizenship if you know why civil service exams are given.

B. WHY ARE CIVIL SERVICE EXAMINATIONS GIVEN?

Civil service examinations are important to you in two ways. As a citizen, you want public jobs filled by employees who know how to do their work. As a job seeker, you want a fair chance to compete for that job on an equal footing with other candidates. The best-known means of accomplishing this two-fold goal is the competitive examination.

Exams are widely publicized throughout the nation. They may be administered for jobs in federal, state, city, municipal, town or village governments or agencies.

Any citizen may apply, with some limitations, such as the age or residence of applicants. Your experience and education may be reviewed to see whether you meet the requirements for the particular examination. When these requirements exist, they are reasonable and applied consistently to all applicants. Thus, a competitive examination may cause you some uneasiness now, but it is your privilege and safeguard.

C. HOW ARE CIVIL SERVICE EXAMS DEVELOPED?

Examinations are carefully written by trained technicians who are specialists in the field known as "psychological measurement," in consultation with recognized authorities in the field of work that the test will cover. These experts recommend the subject matter areas or skills to be tested; only those knowledges or skills important to your success on the job are included. The most reliable books and source materials available are used as references. Together, the experts and technicians judge the difficulty level of the questions.

Test technicians know how to phrase questions so that the problem is clearly stated. Their ethics do not permit "trick" or "catch" questions. Questions may have been tried out on sample groups, or subjected to statistical analysis, to determine their usefulness.

Written tests are often used in combination with performance tests, ratings of training and experience, and oral interviews. All of these measures combine to form the best-known means of finding the right person for the right job.

II. HOW TO PASS THE WRITTEN TEST

A. NATURE OF THE EXAMINATION

To prepare intelligently for civil service examinations, you should know how they differ from school examinations you have taken. In school you were assigned certain definite pages to read or subjects to cover. The examination questions were quite detailed and usually emphasized memory. Civil service exams, on the other hand, try to discover your present ability to perform the duties of a position, plus your potentiality to learn these duties. In other words, a civil service exam attempts to predict how successful you will be. Questions cover such a broad area that they cannot be as minute and detailed as school exam questions.

In the public service similar kinds of work, or positions, are grouped together in one "class." This process is known as *position-classification*. All the positions in a class are paid according to the salary range for that class. One class title covers all of these positions, and they are all tested by the same examination.

B. FOUR BASIC STEPS

1) Study the announcement

How, then, can you know what subjects to study? Our best answer is: "Learn as much as possible about the class of positions for which you've applied." The exam will test the knowledge, skills and abilities needed to do the work.

Your most valuable source of information about the position you want is the official exam announcement. This announcement lists the training and experience qualifications. Check these standards and apply only if you come reasonably close to meeting them.

The brief description of the position in the examination announcement offers some clues to the subjects which will be tested. Think about the job itself. Review the duties in your mind. Can you perform them, or are there some in which you are rusty? Fill in the blank spots in your preparation.

Many jurisdictions preview the written test in the exam announcement by including a section called "Knowledge and Abilities Required," "Scope of the Examination," or some similar heading. Here you will find out specifically what fields will be tested.

2) Review your own background

Once you learn in general what the position is all about, and what you need to know to do the work, ask yourself which subjects you already know fairly well and which need improvement. You may wonder whether to concentrate on improving your strong areas or on building some background in your fields of weakness. When the announcement has specified "some knowledge" or "considerable knowledge," or has used adjectives like "beginning principles of..." or "advanced ... methods," you can get a clue as to the number and difficulty of questions to be asked in any given field. More questions, and hence broader coverage, would be included for those subjects which are more important in the work. Now weigh your strengths and weaknesses against the job requirements and prepare accordingly.

3) Determine the level of the position

Another way to tell how intensively you should prepare is to understand the level of the job for which you are applying. Is it the entering level? In other words, is this the position in which beginners in a field of work are hired? Or is it an intermediate or advanced level? Sometimes this is indicated by such words as "Junior" or "Senior" in the class title. Other jurisdictions use Roman numerals to designate the level – Clerk I, Clerk II, for example. The word "Supervisor" sometimes appears in the title. If the level is not indicated by the title, check the description of duties. Will you be working under very close supervision, or will you have responsibility for independent decisions in this work?

4) Choose appropriate study materials

Now that you know the subjects to be examined and the relative amount of each subject to be covered, you can choose suitable study materials. For beginning level jobs, or even advanced ones, if you have a pronounced weakness in some aspect of your training, read a modern, standard textbook in that field. Be sure it is up to date and has general coverage. Such books are normally available at your library, and the librarian will be glad to help you locate one. For entry-level positions, questions of appropriate difficulty are chosen – neither highly advanced questions, nor those too simple. Such questions require careful thought but not advanced training.

If the position for which you are applying is technical or advanced, you will read more advanced, specialized material. If you are already familiar with the basic principles of your field, elementary textbooks would waste your time. Concentrate on advanced textbooks and technical periodicals. Think through the concepts and review difficult problems in your field.

These are all general sources. You can get more ideas on your own initiative, following these leads. For example, training manuals and publications of the government agency which employs workers in your field can be useful, particularly for technical and professional positions. A letter or visit to the government department involved may result in more specific study suggestions, and certainly will provide you with a more definite idea of the exact nature of the position you are seeking.

III. KINDS OF TESTS

Tests are used for purposes other than measuring knowledge and ability to perform specified duties. For some positions, it is equally important to test ability to make adjustments to new situations or to profit from training. In others, basic mental abilities not dependent on information are essential. Questions which test these things may not appear as pertinent to the duties of the position as those which test for knowledge and information. Yet they are often highly important parts of a fair examination. For very general questions, it is almost impossible to help you direct your study efforts. What we can do is point out some of the more common of these general abilities needed in public service positions and describe some typical questions.

1) General information

Broad, general information has been found useful for predicting job success in some kinds of work. This is tested in a variety of ways, from vocabulary lists to questions about current events. Basic background in some field of work, such as sociology or economics, may be sampled in a group of questions. Often these are principles which have become familiar to most persons through exposure rather than through formal training. It is difficult to advise you how to study for these questions; being alert to the world around you is our best suggestion.

2) Verbal ability

An example of an ability needed in many positions is verbal or language ability. Verbal ability is, in brief, the ability to use and understand words. Vocabulary and grammar tests are typical measures of this ability. Reading comprehension or paragraph interpretation questions are common in many kinds of civil service tests. You are given a paragraph of written material and asked to find its central meaning.

3) Numerical ability

Number skills can be tested by the familiar arithmetic problem, by checking paired lists of numbers to see which are alike and which are different, or by interpreting charts and graphs. In the latter test, a graph may be printed in the test booklet which you are asked to use as the basis for answering questions.

4) Observation

A popular test for law-enforcement positions is the observation test. A picture is shown to you for several minutes, then taken away. Questions about the picture test your ability to observe both details and larger elements.

5) Following directions

In many positions in the public service, the employee must be able to carry out written instructions dependably and accurately. You may be given a chart with several columns, each column listing a variety of information. The questions require you to carry out directions involving the information given in the chart.

6) Skills and aptitudes

Performance tests effectively measure some manual skills and aptitudes. When the skill is one in which you are trained, such as typing or shorthand, you can practice. These tests are often very much like those given in business school or high school courses. For many of the other skills and aptitudes, however, no short-time preparation can be made. Skills and abilities natural to you or that you have developed throughout your lifetime are being tested.

Many of the general questions just described provide all the data needed to answer the questions and ask you to use your reasoning ability to find the answers. Your best preparation for these tests, as well as for tests of facts and ideas, is to be at your physical and mental best. You, no doubt, have your own methods of getting into an exam-taking mood and keeping "in shape." The next section lists some ideas on this subject.

IV. KINDS OF QUESTIONS

Only rarely is the "essay" question, which you answer in narrative form, used in civil service tests. Civil service tests are usually of the short-answer type. Full instructions for answering these questions will be given to you at the examination. But in case this is your first experience with short-answer questions and separate answer sheets, here is what you need to know:

1) Multiple-choice Questions

Most popular of the short-answer questions is the "multiple choice" or "best answer" question. It can be used, for example, to test for factual knowledge, ability to solve problems or judgment in meeting situations found at work.

A multiple-choice question is normally one of three types—
- It can begin with an incomplete statement followed by several possible endings. You are to find the one ending which *best* completes the statement, although some of the others may not be entirely wrong.
- It can also be a complete statement in the form of a question which is answered by choosing one of the statements listed.

- It can be in the form of a problem – again you select the best answer.

Here is an example of a multiple-choice question with a discussion which should give you some clues as to the method for choosing the right answer:

When an employee has a complaint about his assignment, the action which will *best* help him overcome his difficulty is to
   A. discuss his difficulty with his coworkers
   B. take the problem to the head of the organization
   C. take the problem to the person who gave him the assignment
   D. say nothing to anyone about his complaint

In answering this question, you should study each of the choices to find which is best. Consider choice "A" – Certainly an employee may discuss his complaint with fellow employees, but no change or improvement can result, and the complaint remains unresolved. Choice "B" is a poor choice since the head of the organization probably does not know what assignment you have been given, and taking your problem to him is known as "going over the head" of the supervisor. The supervisor, or person who made the assignment, is the person who can clarify it or correct any injustice. Choice "C" is, therefore, correct. To say nothing, as in choice "D," is unwise. Supervisors have and interest in knowing the problems employees are facing, and the employee is seeking a solution to his problem.

2) True/False Questions

The "true/false" or "right/wrong" form of question is sometimes used. Here a complete statement is given. Your job is to decide whether the statement is right or wrong.

SAMPLE: A roaming cell-phone call to a nearby city costs less than a non-roaming call to a distant city.

This statement is wrong, or false, since roaming calls are more expensive.
This is not a complete list of all possible question forms, although most of the others are variations of these common types. You will always get complete directions for answering questions. Be sure you understand *how* to mark your answers – ask questions until you do.

V. RECORDING YOUR ANSWERS

Computer terminals are used more and more today for many different kinds of exams.
For an examination with very few applicants, you may be told to record your answers in the test booklet itself. Separate answer sheets are much more common. If this separate answer sheet is to be scored by machine – and this is often the case – it is highly important that you mark your answers correctly in order to get credit.
An electronic scoring machine is often used in civil service offices because of the speed with which papers can be scored. Machine-scored answer sheets must be marked with a pencil, which will be given to you. This pencil has a high graphite content which responds to the electronic scoring machine. As a matter of fact, stray dots may register as answers, so do not let your pencil rest on the answer sheet while you are pondering the correct answer. Also, if your pencil lead breaks or is otherwise defective, ask for another.

Since the answer sheet will be dropped in a slot in the scoring machine, be careful not to bend the corners or get the paper crumpled.

The answer sheet normally has five vertical columns of numbers, with 30 numbers to a column. These numbers correspond to the question numbers in your test booklet. After each number, going across the page are four or five pairs of dotted lines. These short dotted lines have small letters or numbers above them. The first two pairs may also have a "T" or "F" above the letters. This indicates that the first two pairs only are to be used if the questions are of the true-false type. If the questions are multiple choice, disregard the "T" and "F" and pay attention only to the small letters or numbers.

Answer your questions in the manner of the sample that follows:

32. The largest city in the United States is
    A. Washington, D.C.
    B. New York City
    C. Chicago
    D. Detroit
    E. San Francisco

1) Choose the answer you think is best. (New York City is the largest, so "B" is correct.)
2) Find the row of dotted lines numbered the same as the question you are answering. (Find row number 32)
3) Find the pair of dotted lines corresponding to the answer. (Find the pair of lines under the mark "B.")
4) Make a solid black mark between the dotted lines.

VI. BEFORE THE TEST

Common sense will help you find procedures to follow to get ready for an examination. Too many of us, however, overlook these sensible measures. Indeed, nervousness and fatigue have been found to be the most serious reasons why applicants fail to do their best on civil service tests. Here is a list of reminders:

- Begin your preparation early – Don't wait until the last minute to go scurrying around for books and materials or to find out what the position is all about.
- Prepare continuously – An hour a night for a week is better than an all-night cram session. This has been definitely established. What is more, a night a week for a month will return better dividends than crowding your study into a shorter period of time.
- Locate the place of the exam – You have been sent a notice telling you when and where to report for the examination. If the location is in a different town or otherwise unfamiliar to you, it would be well to inquire the best route and learn something about the building.
- Relax the night before the test – Allow your mind to rest. Do not study at all that night. Plan some mild recreation or diversion; then go to bed early and get a good night's sleep.
- Get up early enough to make a leisurely trip to the place for the test – This way unforeseen events, traffic snarls, unfamiliar buildings, etc. will not upset you.
- Dress comfortably – A written test is not a fashion show. You will be known by number and not by name, so wear something comfortable.

- Leave excess paraphernalia at home – Shopping bags and odd bundles will get in your way. You need bring only the items mentioned in the official notice you received; usually everything you need is provided. Do not bring reference books to the exam. They will only confuse those last minutes and be taken away from you when in the test room.
- Arrive somewhat ahead of time – If because of transportation schedules you must get there very early, bring a newspaper or magazine to take your mind off yourself while waiting.
- Locate the examination room – When you have found the proper room, you will be directed to the seat or part of the room where you will sit. Sometimes you are given a sheet of instructions to read while you are waiting. Do not fill out any forms until you are told to do so; just read them and be prepared.
- Relax and prepare to listen to the instructions
- If you have any physical problem that may keep you from doing your best, be sure to tell the test administrator. If you are sick or in poor health, you really cannot do your best on the exam. You can come back and take the test some other time.

VII. AT THE TEST

The day of the test is here and you have the test booklet in your hand. The temptation to get going is very strong. Caution! There is more to success than knowing the right answers. You must know how to identify your papers and understand variations in the type of short-answer question used in this particular examination. Follow these suggestions for maximum results from your efforts:

1) Cooperate with the monitor

The test administrator has a duty to create a situation in which you can be as much at ease as possible. He will give instructions, tell you when to begin, check to see that you are marking your answer sheet correctly, and so on. He is not there to guard you, although he will see that your competitors do not take unfair advantage. He wants to help you do your best.

2) Listen to all instructions

Don't jump the gun! Wait until you understand all directions. In most civil service tests you get more time than you need to answer the questions. So don't be in a hurry. Read each word of instructions until you clearly understand the meaning. Study the examples, listen to all announcements and follow directions. Ask questions if you do not understand what to do.

3) Identify your papers

Civil service exams are usually identified by number only. You will be assigned a number; you must not put your name on your test papers. Be sure to copy your number correctly. Since more than one exam may be given, copy your exact examination title.

4) Plan your time

Unless you are told that a test is a "speed" or "rate of work" test, speed itself is usually not important. Time enough to answer all the questions will be provided, but this does not mean that you have all day. An overall time limit has been set. Divide the total time (in minutes) by the number of questions to determine the approximate time you have for each question.

5) Do not linger over difficult questions

If you come across a difficult question, mark it with a paper clip (useful to have along) and come back to it when you have been through the booklet. One caution if you do this – be sure to skip a number on your answer sheet as well. Check often to be sure that you have not lost your place and that you are marking in the row numbered the same as the question you are answering.

6) Read the questions

Be sure you know what the question asks! Many capable people are unsuccessful because they failed to *read* the questions correctly.

7) Answer all questions

Unless you have been instructed that a penalty will be deducted for incorrect answers, it is better to guess than to omit a question.

8) Speed tests

It is often better NOT to guess on speed tests. It has been found that on timed tests people are tempted to spend the last few seconds before time is called in marking answers at random – without even reading them – in the hope of picking up a few extra points. To discourage this practice, the instructions may warn you that your score will be "corrected" for guessing. That is, a penalty will be applied. The incorrect answers will be deducted from the correct ones, or some other penalty formula will be used.

9) Review your answers

If you finish before time is called, go back to the questions you guessed or omitted to give them further thought. Review other answers if you have time.

10) Return your test materials

If you are ready to leave before others have finished or time is called, take ALL your materials to the monitor and leave quietly. Never take any test material with you. The monitor can discover whose papers are not complete, and taking a test booklet may be grounds for disqualification.

VIII. EXAMINATION TECHNIQUES

1) Read the general instructions carefully. These are usually printed on the first page of the exam booklet. As a rule, these instructions refer to the timing of the examination; the fact that you should not start work until the signal and must stop work at a signal, etc. If there are any *special* instructions, such as a choice of questions to be answered, make sure that you note this instruction carefully.

2) When you are ready to start work on the examination, that is as soon as the signal has been given, read the instructions to each question booklet, underline any key words or phrases, such as *least, best, outline, describe* and the like. In this way you will tend to answer as requested rather than discover on reviewing your paper that you *listed without describing*, that you selected the *worst* choice rather than the *best* choice, etc.

3) If the examination is of the objective or multiple-choice type – that is, each question will also give a series of possible answers: A, B, C or D, and you are called upon to select the best answer and write the letter next to that answer on your answer paper – it is advisable to start answering each question in turn. There may be anywhere from 50 to 100 such questions in the three or four hours allotted and you can see how much time would be taken if you read through all the questions before beginning to answer any. Furthermore, if you come across a question or group of questions which you know would be difficult to answer, it would undoubtedly affect your handling of all the other questions.

4) If the examination is of the essay type and contains but a few questions, it is a moot point as to whether you should read all the questions before starting to answer any one. Of course, if you are given a choice – say five out of seven and the like – then it is essential to read all the questions so you can eliminate the two that are most difficult. If, however, you are asked to answer all the questions, there may be danger in trying to answer the easiest one first because you may find that you will spend too much time on it. The best technique is to answer the first question, then proceed to the second, etc.

5) Time your answers. Before the exam begins, write down the time it started, then add the time allowed for the examination and write down the time it must be completed, then divide the time available somewhat as follows:
    - If 3-1/2 hours are allowed, that would be 210 minutes. If you have 80 objective-type questions, that would be an average of 2-1/2 minutes per question. Allow yourself no more than 2 minutes per question, or a total of 160 minutes, which will permit about 50 minutes to review.
    - If for the time allotment of 210 minutes there are 7 essay questions to answer, that would average about 30 minutes a question. Give yourself only 25 minutes per question so that you have about 35 minutes to review.

6) The most important instruction is to *read each question* and make sure you know what is wanted. The second most important instruction is to *time yourself properly* so that you answer every question. The third most important instruction is to *answer every question*. Guess if you have to but include something for each question. Remember that you will receive no credit for a blank and will probably receive some credit if you write something in answer to an essay question. If you guess a letter – say "B" for a multiple-choice question – you may have guessed right. If you leave a blank as an answer to a multiple-choice question, the examiners may respect your feelings but it will not add a point to your score. Some exams may penalize you for wrong answers, so in such cases *only*, you may not want to guess unless you have some basis for your answer.

7) Suggestions
    a. Objective-type questions
        1. Examine the question booklet for proper sequence of pages and questions
        2. Read all instructions carefully
        3. Skip any question which seems too difficult; return to it after all other questions have been answered
        4. Apportion your time properly; do not spend too much time on any single question or group of questions

5. Note and underline key words – *all, most, fewest, least, best, worst, same, opposite,* etc.
6. Pay particular attention to negatives
7. Note unusual option, e.g., unduly long, short, complex, different or similar in content to the body of the question
8. Observe the use of "hedging" words – *probably, may, most likely,* etc.
9. Make sure that your answer is put next to the same number as the question
10. Do not second-guess unless you have good reason to believe the second answer is definitely more correct
11. Cross out original answer if you decide another answer is more accurate; do not erase until you are ready to hand your paper in
12. Answer all questions; guess unless instructed otherwise
13. Leave time for review

b. Essay questions
1. Read each question carefully
2. Determine exactly what is wanted. Underline key words or phrases.
3. Decide on outline or paragraph answer
4. Include many different points and elements unless asked to develop any one or two points or elements
5. Show impartiality by giving pros and cons unless directed to select one side only
6. Make and write down any assumptions you find necessary to answer the questions
7. Watch your English, grammar, punctuation and choice of words
8. Time your answers; don't crowd material

8) Answering the essay question

Most essay questions can be answered by framing the specific response around several key words or ideas. Here are a few such key words or ideas:

M's: manpower, materials, methods, money, management
P's: purpose, program, policy, plan, procedure, practice, problems, pitfalls, personnel, public relations

a. Six basic steps in handling problems:
1. Preliminary plan and background development
2. Collect information, data and facts
3. Analyze and interpret information, data and facts
4. Analyze and develop solutions as well as make recommendations
5. Prepare report and sell recommendations
6. Install recommendations and follow up effectiveness

b. Pitfalls to avoid
1. *Taking things for granted* – A statement of the situation does not necessarily imply that each of the elements is necessarily true; for example, a complaint may be invalid and biased so that all that can be taken for granted is that a complaint has been registered

2. *Considering only one side of a situation* – Wherever possible, indicate several alternatives and then point out the reasons you selected the best one
3. *Failing to indicate follow up* – Whenever your answer indicates action on your part, make certain that you will take proper follow-up action to see how successful your recommendations, procedures or actions turn out to be
4. *Taking too long in answering any single question* – Remember to time your answers properly

IX. AFTER THE TEST

Scoring procedures differ in detail among civil service jurisdictions although the general principles are the same. Whether the papers are hand-scored or graded by machine we have described, they are nearly always graded by number. That is, the person who marks the paper knows only the number – never the name – of the applicant. Not until all the papers have been graded will they be matched with names. If other tests, such as training and experience or oral interview ratings have been given, scores will be combined. Different parts of the examination usually have different weights. For example, the written test might count 60 percent of the final grade, and a rating of training and experience 40 percent. In many jurisdictions, veterans will have a certain number of points added to their grades.

After the final grade has been determined, the names are placed in grade order and an eligible list is established. There are various methods for resolving ties between those who get the same final grade – probably the most common is to place first the name of the person whose application was received first. Job offers are made from the eligible list in the order the names appear on it. You will be notified of your grade and your rank as soon as all these computations have been made. This will be done as rapidly as possible.

People who are found to meet the requirements in the announcement are called "eligibles." Their names are put on a list of eligible candidates. An eligible's chances of getting a job depend on how high he stands on this list and how fast agencies are filling jobs from the list.

When a job is to be filled from a list of eligibles, the agency asks for the names of people on the list of eligibles for that job. When the civil service commission receives this request, it sends to the agency the names of the three people highest on this list. Or, if the job to be filled has specialized requirements, the office sends the agency the names of the top three persons who meet these requirements from the general list.

The appointing officer makes a choice from among the three people whose names were sent to him. If the selected person accepts the appointment, the names of the others are put back on the list to be considered for future openings.

That is the rule in hiring from all kinds of eligible lists, whether they are for typist, carpenter, chemist, or something else. For every vacancy, the appointing officer has his choice of any one of the top three eligibles on the list. This explains why the person whose name is on top of the list sometimes does not get an appointment when some of the persons lower on the list do. If the appointing officer chooses the second or third eligible, the No. 1 eligible does not get a job at once, but stays on the list until he is appointed or the list is terminated.

X. HOW TO PASS THE INTERVIEW TEST

The examination for which you applied requires an oral interview test. You have already taken the written test and you are now being called for the interview test – the final part of the formal examination.

You may think that it is not possible to prepare for an interview test and that there are no procedures to follow during an interview. Our purpose is to point out some things you can do in advance that will help you and some good rules to follow and pitfalls to avoid while you are being interviewed.

What is an interview supposed to test?

The written examination is designed to test the technical knowledge and competence of the candidate; the oral is designed to evaluate intangible qualities, not readily measured otherwise, and to establish a list showing the relative fitness of each candidate – as measured against his competitors – for the position sought. Scoring is not on the basis of "right" and "wrong," but on a sliding scale of values ranging from "not passable" to "outstanding." As a matter of fact, it is possible to achieve a relatively low score without a single "incorrect" answer because of evident weakness in the qualities being measured.

Occasionally, an examination may consist entirely of an oral test – either an individual or a group oral. In such cases, information is sought concerning the technical knowledges and abilities of the candidate, since there has been no written examination for this purpose. More commonly, however, an oral test is used to supplement a written examination.

Who conducts interviews?

The composition of oral boards varies among different jurisdictions. In nearly all, a representative of the personnel department serves as chairman. One of the members of the board may be a representative of the department in which the candidate would work. In some cases, "outside experts" are used, and, frequently, a businessman or some other representative of the general public is asked to serve. Labor and management or other special groups may be represented. The aim is to secure the services of experts in the appropriate field.

However the board is composed, it is a good idea (and not at all improper or unethical) to ascertain in advance of the interview who the members are and what groups they represent. When you are introduced to them, you will have some idea of their backgrounds and interests, and at least you will not stutter and stammer over their names.

What should be done before the interview?

While knowledge about the board members is useful and takes some of the surprise element out of the interview, there is other preparation which is more substantive. It *is* possible to prepare for an oral interview – in several ways:

1) Keep a copy of your application and review it carefully before the interview

This may be the only document before the oral board, and the starting point of the interview. Know what education and experience you have listed there, and the sequence and dates of all of it. Sometimes the board will ask you to review the highlights of your experience for them; you should not have to hem and haw doing it.

2) Study the class specification and the examination announcement

Usually, the oral board has one or both of these to guide them. The qualities, characteristics or knowledges required by the position sought are stated in these documents. They offer valuable clues as to the nature of the oral interview. For example, if the job involves supervisory responsibilities, the announcement will usually indicate that knowledge of modern supervisory methods and the qualifications of the candidate as a supervisor will be tested. If so, you can expect such questions, frequently in the form of a hypothetical situation which you are expected to solve. NEVER go into an oral without knowledge of the duties and responsibilities of the job you seek.

3) Think through each qualification required

Try to visualize the kind of questions you would ask if you were a board member. How well could you answer them? Try especially to appraise your own knowledge and background in each area, *measured against the job sought*, and identify any areas in which you are weak. Be critical and realistic – do not flatter yourself.

4) Do some general reading in areas in which you feel you may be weak

For example, if the job involves supervision and your past experience has NOT, some general reading in supervisory methods and practices, particularly in the field of human relations, might be useful. Do NOT study agency procedures or detailed manuals. The oral board will be testing your understanding and capacity, not your memory.

5) Get a good night's sleep and watch your general health and mental attitude

You will want a clear head at the interview. Take care of a cold or any other minor ailment, and of course, no hangovers.

What should be done on the day of the interview?

Now comes the day of the interview itself. Give yourself plenty of time to get there. Plan to arrive somewhat ahead of the scheduled time, particularly if your appointment is in the fore part of the day. If a previous candidate fails to appear, the board might be ready for you a bit early. By early afternoon an oral board is almost invariably behind schedule if there are many candidates, and you may have to wait. Take along a book or magazine to read, or your application to review, but leave any extraneous material in the waiting room when you go in for your interview. In any event, relax and compose yourself.

The matter of dress is important. The board is forming impressions about you – from your experience, your manners, your attitude, and your appearance. Give your personal appearance careful attention. Dress your best, but not your flashiest. Choose conservative, appropriate clothing, and be sure it is immaculate. This is a business interview, and your appearance should indicate that you regard it as such. Besides, being well groomed and properly dressed will help boost your confidence.

Sooner or later, someone will call your name and escort you into the interview room. *This is it.* From here on you are on your own. It is too late for any more preparation. But remember, you asked for this opportunity to prove your fitness, and you are here because your request was granted.

What happens when you go in?

The usual sequence of events will be as follows: The clerk (who is often the board stenographer) will introduce you to the chairman of the oral board, who will introduce you to the other members of the board. Acknowledge the introductions before you sit down. Do not be surprised if you find a microphone facing you or a stenotypist sitting by. Oral interviews are usually recorded in the event of an appeal or other review.

Usually the chairman of the board will open the interview by reviewing the highlights of your education and work experience from your application – primarily for the benefit of the other members of the board, as well as to get the material into the record. Do not interrupt or comment unless there is an error or significant misinterpretation; if that is the case, do not hesitate. But do not quibble about insignificant matters. Also, he will usually ask you some question about your education, experience or your present job – partly to get you to start talking and to establish the interviewing "rapport." He may start the actual questioning, or turn it over to one of the other members. Frequently, each member undertakes the questioning on a particular area, one in which he is perhaps most competent, so you can expect each member to participate in the examination. Because time is limited, you may also expect some rather abrupt switches in the direction the questioning takes, so do not be upset by it. Normally, a board member will not pursue a single line of questioning unless he discovers a particular strength or weakness.

After each member has participated, the chairman will usually ask whether any member has any further questions, then will ask you if you have anything you wish to add. Unless you are expecting this question, it may floor you. Worse, it may start you off on an extended, extemporaneous speech. The board is not usually seeking more information. The question is principally to offer you a last opportunity to present further qualifications or to indicate that you have nothing to add. So, if you feel that a significant qualification or characteristic has been overlooked, it is proper to point it out in a sentence or so. Do not compliment the board on the thoroughness of their examination – they have been sketchy, and you know it. If you wish, merely say, "No thank you, I have nothing further to add." This is a point where you can "talk yourself out" of a good impression or fail to present an important bit of information. Remember, *you close the interview yourself.*

The chairman will then say, "That is all, Mr. _____, thank you." Do not be startled; the interview is over, and quicker than you think. Thank him, gather your belongings and take your leave. Save your sigh of relief for the other side of the door.

How to put your best foot forward

Throughout this entire process, you may feel that the board individually and collectively is trying to pierce your defenses, seek out your hidden weaknesses and embarrass and confuse you. Actually, this is not true. They are obliged to make an appraisal of your qualifications for the job you are seeking, and they want to see you in your best light. Remember, they must interview all candidates and a non-cooperative candidate may become a failure in spite of their best efforts to bring out his qualifications. Here are 15 suggestions that will help you:

1) Be natural – Keep your attitude confident, not cocky

If you are not confident that you can do the job, do not expect the board to be. Do not apologize for your weaknesses, try to bring out your strong points. The board is interested in a positive, not negative, presentation. Cockiness will antagonize any board member and make him wonder if you are covering up a weakness by a false show of strength.

2) Get comfortable, but don't lounge or sprawl

Sit erectly but not stiffly. A careless posture may lead the board to conclude that you are careless in other things, or at least that you are not impressed by the importance of the occasion. Either conclusion is natural, even if incorrect. Do not fuss with your clothing, a pencil or an ashtray. Your hands may occasionally be useful to emphasize a point; do not let them become a point of distraction.

3) Do not wisecrack or make small talk

This is a serious situation, and your attitude should show that you consider it as such. Further, the time of the board is limited – they do not want to waste it, and neither should you.

4) Do not exaggerate your experience or abilities

In the first place, from information in the application or other interviews and sources, the board may know more about you than you think. Secondly, you probably will not get away with it. An experienced board is rather adept at spotting such a situation, so do not take the chance.

5) If you know a board member, do not make a point of it, yet do not hide it

Certainly you are not fooling him, and probably not the other members of the board. Do not try to take advantage of your acquaintanceship – it will probably do you little good.

6) Do not dominate the interview

Let the board do that. They will give you the clues – do not assume that you have to do all the talking. Realize that the board has a number of questions to ask you, and do not try to take up all the interview time by showing off your extensive knowledge of the answer to the first one.

7) Be attentive

You only have 20 minutes or so, and you should keep your attention at its sharpest throughout. When a member is addressing a problem or question to you, give him your undivided attention. Address your reply principally to him, but do not exclude the other board members.

8) Do not interrupt

A board member may be stating a problem for you to analyze. He will ask you a question when the time comes. Let him state the problem, and wait for the question.

9) Make sure you understand the question

Do not try to answer until you are sure what the question is. If it is not clear, restate it in your own words or ask the board member to clarify it for you. However, do not haggle about minor elements.

10) Reply promptly but not hastily

A common entry on oral board rating sheets is "candidate responded readily," or "candidate hesitated in replies." Respond as promptly and quickly as you can, but do not jump to a hasty, ill-considered answer.

11) Do not be peremptory in your answers

A brief answer is proper – but do not fire your answer back. That is a losing game from your point of view. The board member can probably ask questions much faster than you can answer them.

12) Do not try to create the answer you think the board member wants

He is interested in what kind of mind you have and how it works – not in playing games. Furthermore, he can usually spot this practice and will actually grade you down on it.

13) Do not switch sides in your reply merely to agree with a board member

Frequently, a member will take a contrary position merely to draw you out and to see if you are willing and able to defend your point of view. Do not start a debate, yet do not surrender a good position. If a position is worth taking, it is worth defending.

14) Do not be afraid to admit an error in judgment if you are shown to be wrong

The board knows that you are forced to reply without any opportunity for careful consideration. Your answer may be demonstrably wrong. If so, admit it and get on with the interview.

15) Do not dwell at length on your present job

The opening question may relate to your present assignment. Answer the question but do not go into an extended discussion. You are being examined for a *new* job, not your present one. As a matter of fact, try to phrase ALL your answers in terms of the job for which you are being examined.

Basis of Rating

Probably you will forget most of these "do's" and "don'ts" when you walk into the oral interview room. Even remembering them all will not ensure you a passing grade. Perhaps you did not have the qualifications in the first place. But remembering them will help you to put your best foot forward, without treading on the toes of the board members.

Rumor and popular opinion to the contrary notwithstanding, an oral board wants you to make the best appearance possible. They know you are under pressure – but they also want to see how you respond to it as a guide to what your reaction would be under the pressures of the job you seek. They will be influenced by the degree of poise you display, the personal traits you show and the manner in which you respond.

ABOUT THIS BOOK

This book contains tests divided into Examination Sections. Go through each test, answering every question in the margin. We have also attached a sample answer sheet at the back of the book that can be removed and used. At the end of each test look at the answer key and check your answers. On the ones you got wrong, look at the right answer choice and learn. Do not fill in the answers first. Do not memorize the questions and answers, but understand the answer and principles involved. On your test, the questions will likely be different from the samples. Questions are changed and new ones added. If you understand these past questions you should have success with any changes that arise. Tests may consist of several types of questions. We have additional books on each subject should more study be advisable or necessary for you. Finally, the more you study, the better prepared you will be. This book is intended to be the last thing you study before you walk into the examination room. Prior study of relevant texts is also recommended. NLC publishes some of these in our Fundamental Series. Knowledge and good sense are important factors in passing your exam. Good luck also helps. So now study this Passbook, absorb the material contained within and take that knowledge into the examination. Then do your best to pass that exam.

EXAMINATION SECTION

EXAMINATION SECTION
TEST 1

DIRECTIONS: Each question or incomplete statement is followed by several suggested answers or completions. Select the one that BEST answers the question or completes the statement. *PRINT THE LETTER OF THE CORRECT ANSWER IN THE SPACE AT THE RIGHT.*

1. Of the following brushes, the one that is USUALLY used to apply acoustic plaster, and then to punch the surface to make an evenly textured surface is a _____ brush.

   A. wire   B. B, scrub   C. dash   D. stippling

   1.____

2. A tool about 6 feet long and 5 inches wide, used to straighten angles (corners) in the finish coat of plaster, is a

   A. rod   B. slicker
   C. featheredge   D. darby

   2.____

3. A material used to make bristles for plasterers finishing brushes is

   A. sisal   B. nylon
   C. prestressed wire   D. palmetto

   3.____

4. The PRIMARY requirement of a browning brush is that it be

   A. made with a very long handle
   B. made with very rigid bristles
   C. capable of holding a large amount of water
   D. at least 2 1/2 inches by 6 inches in size

   4.____

5. A 12-inch by 6-inch hawk with a lip on one side and a handle fastened to the underside is known as a(n)

   A. jack hawk   B. corner maker
   C. mud holder   D. arris maker

   5.____

6. Of the following tools, the one that should be used to break up lumps in a lime putty mix is a

   A. vibrator   B. hoe   C. paddle   D. scratcher

   6.____

7. A small trowel used for cleaning plastering tools and for small plastering jobs is a _____ trowel.

   A. panel   B. corner   C. joint   D. pointing

   7.____

8. A hood carrier's ladder differs from an ordinary ladder mainly in that it has

   A. less space between the rungs than an ordinary ladder
   B. more space between the rungs than an ordinary ladder
   C. a rail in the middle for extra strength
   D. a hand rail on the left side

   8.____

9. A lathing hatchet *differs* from an ordinary hatchet mainly in that a lathing hatchet has a

    A. shorter handle with a thinner grip
    B. cross-hatched head with grooves and a thicker grip
    C. steel reinforced wood handle with a rubber grip
    D. shorter head and a shorter handle

10. Angle floats are LEAST likely to be made of

    A. plexiglass   B. stainless steel
    C. duriron   D. aluminum

11. The one of the following that is NOT a cementing material is

    A. lime   B. plaster of Paris
    C. perlite   D. gypsum

12. Gypsum board lath is made

    A. both in plain and perforated boards
    B. both in perforated and corrugated boards
    C. in plain boards only
    D. in perforated boards only

13. Of the following, the BEST reason for galvanizing steel furring is to _____ of the steel furring

    A. reduce the expansion and contraction
    B. prevent corrosion
    C. increase the roughness
    D. reduce the deflection

14. When properly applied by a plasterer, Keene's cement plaster sets _____ with a _____ surface.

    A. *quickly;* smooth   B. *quickly;* rough
    C. *slowly;* smooth   D. *slowly;* rough

15. A cubic foot of vermiculite used in plastering weighs MOST NEARLY _____ pounds.

    A. 10   B. 20   C. 40   D. 80

16. Of the following, the material that is NOT used in plastering is

    A. foamed slag   B. perlite
    C. pumice   D. permutite

17. Of the following, the one which is NOT considered to be a cementing agent is

    A. gypsum   B. rosin
    C. lime   D. Portland cement

18. The ability of a masonry base to absorb moisture from plaster applied directly to the base is known as

    A. dilution   B. dehydration
    C. suction   D. saturation

19. Of the following methods, the one that is LEAST likely to be used for the purpose of squaring a room before applying the plaster is the _____ method.
    A. right-angle triangle
    B. square
    C. center-line
    D. diagonal-line

20. In three-coat plaster work, the second coat of plaster is known as the _____ coat.
    A. scratch   B. base   C. brown   D. finish

21. The LOWEST temperature at which plaster may be applied to a wall is _____ F.
    A. 25   B. 32   C. 40   D. 50

22. A material which will *shorten* the time it takes for plaster to set is
    A. zeolite
    B. set gypsum
    C. calcite
    D. sulphate of zinc

23. When darbying a wall, the plasterer should start at
    A. the bottom of the wall and work upward
    B. the top of the wall and work downward
    C. the center of the wall and work upward and downward
    D. an upper corner of the wall and work diagonally to the opposite corner

24. The addition of plaster of Paris gypsum to mortar to make the mortar set more quickly is called
    A. fluxing   B. retarding   C. sizing   D. gauging

25. Of the following, the material which will expand or shrink the LEAST upon setting is
    A. uniformly applied Bond plaster
    B. thickly applied Keene's cement
    C. a rich, uniform, Portland cement mixture
    D. a rich lime mortar mixture

KEY (CORRECT ANSWERS)

1.	D	11.	C
2.	C	12.	A
3.	B	13.	B
4.	C	14.	A
5.	C	15.	A
6.	B	16.	D
7.	D	17.	B
8.	A	18.	C
9.	B	19.	D
10.	C	20.	C

21. C
22. B
23. A
24. D
25. A

TEST 2

DIRECTIONS: Each question or incomplete statement is followed by several suggested answers or completions. Select the one that BEST answers the question or completes the statement. *PRINT THE LETTER OF THE CORRECT ANSWER IN THE SPACE AT THE RIGHT.*

1. A brick wall shows a whitish deposit on it.
   Before plastering the wall, it should be cleaned FIRST with a wire brush and then washed with a _____ solution.

   A. gasoline
   B. tri-sodium phosphate
   C. muriatic acid
   D. copper sulphate

2. *Doubling-up* or *doubling-back* is a method of applying the

   A. wire lath
   B. brown coat
   C. cornice
   D. white coat

3. A putty ring is *usually* formed on a

   A. beam soffit
   B. lintel
   C. finishing board
   D. scuttle

4. Of the following areas, the one where Portland cement plaster is MOST likely to be used in preference to gypsum plaster is on a(n) _____ wall.

   A. kitchen closet
   B. clothes closet
   C. shower stall
   D. outside

5. Of the following gypsum mortar mixes, the mix that should be applied DIRECTLY on a soft common brick surface is _____ to 1.

   A. 3 1/2   B. 2 1/4   C. 1 1/2   D. 3/4

6. Of the following, the PROPER mix for Portland cement mortar is _____ parts _____ to 1 part _____.

   A. 3; sand; cement
   B. 2; sand; cement
   C. 3; cement; sand
   D. 2; cement; sand

7. In order to prevent the finished surface of a plastered wall from cracking, the MINIMUM thickness of a Keene's cement finish coat that should be applied is

   A. 1/32"   B. 1/8"   C. 1/4"   D. 3/8"

8. A snail amount of plaster placed on a ceiling to serve as a thickness guide for applying the remainder of the plaster is USUALLY called a

   A. key   B. ground   C. screed   D. base

9. After each trowelful of mortar is lifted from a hawk, the hawk should be rotated a _____ turn.

   A. one-eighth
   B. one-quarter
   C. three-eighths
   D. one-half

10. When applying a scratch coat to a diamond-mesh metal lath, the trowel should be held _____ and _____ pressure should be applied.   10.____

   A. horizontally; heavy
   B. at an angle; light
   C. at an angle; heavy
   D. vertically; light

11. On better class plaster work, the FIRST step in establishing a screed on a wall is to   11.____

   A. set a water level line
   B. stretch a chalk line from wall to wall
   C. place some plaster dots of the required thickness on the wall
   D. nail the cornice in place

12. Fibered mortar would MOST likely be used for a scratch coat that is to be applied to   12.____

   A. woven-wire lath
   B. wood lath
   C. a concrete base
   D. perforated gypsum board lath

13. The LEAST likely reason to add an admixture to a plaster mix is to   13.____

   A. increase its workability
   B. change the setting time
   C. increase its strength
   D. add color to the mortar

14. Acoustic plaster is USUALLY applied in   14.____

   A. one 3/4-inch coat only
   B. one 1/2-inch coat only
   C. two 3/8-inch coats
   D. two 1/4-inch coats

15. A scratch coat would usually NOT be applied to   15.____

   A. insulating board lath
   B. wood lath
   C. cement block
   D. gypsum lath

16. In order to cure stucco under normal weather conditions, the brown and finish coats should be kept continuously _____ for a minimum of _____ day(s).   16.____

   A. soaked; 3
   B. damp; 2
   C. soaked; 2
   D. damp; 1

17. When a plaster mix contains more gypsum than is normal, it is known as a _____ mix.   17.____

   A. fat   B. lean   C. rich   D. white

18. After the initial darbying of a plastered wall, the hollow spots that show up are filled in with mortar. The next step, before the second darbying, is to sprinkle water on the surface of the plaster.   18.____
   The MAIN purpose of this water is to

   A. kill the plaster
   B. retard the set
   C. act as a lubricant
   D. dissolve the scum on the wall

19. The FIRST step in plastering an exposed steel beam after the metal lath is in place is to

    A. strip the beam
    B. set the plaster dots
    C. establish a water-level line
    D. apply the scratch coat

20. Strips of wood used as thickness guides and to stop plastering around door and window openings are known as

    A. cleats
    B. batter boards
    C. shims
    D. grounds

21. Which of the following options CORRECTLY lists the order in which the various parts of a room with a high ceiling should be plastered?

    A. Entire ceiling, bottom part of wall, top part of wall
    B. Entire ceiling, top part of wall, bottom part of wall
    C. Bottom part of wall, top part of wall, ceiling
    D. Top part of wall, bottom part of wall, ceiling

22. An *advantage* of a Keene's cement finish over a putty coat finish is that it

    A. sets faster
    B. is harder
    C. requires less mixing
    D. takes less time to apply

23. The REASON for scratching the first coat of mortar in a 3-coat plaster job is to

    A. provide a mechanical key for the next coat
    B. increase the base suction
    C. adjust for unevenness in the base coat
    D. provide more drying area

24. Travertine finish on a plaster surface is formed by using a trowel and a

    A. whisk broom
    B. sponge
    C. stippling brush
    D. tool brush

25. One advantage of a sand finish over a putty coat is that the sand finish

    A. uses more readily available material
    B. may be applied over a wet brown coat
    C. does not have to be floated
    D. is more uniform in application

KEY (CORRECT ANSWERS)

1. C
2. B
3. C
4. D
5. A

6. A
7. B
8. C
9. B
10. B

11. C
12. A
13. A
14. D
15. C

16. B
17. C
18. C
19. D
20. D

21. B
22. B
23. A
24. A
25. B

TEST 3

DIRECTIONS: Each question or incomplete statement is followed by several suggested answers or completions. Select the one that BEST answers the question or completes the statement. *PRINT THE LETTER OF THE CORRECT ANSWER IN THE SPACE AT THE RIGHT.*

1. In general, scratch coat mortar to be applied to metal lathing should be _____ and _____.   1._____

    A. stiff; rich
    B. loose; rich
    C. stiff; lean
    D. loose; lean

2. The scratch coat of gypsum that would require the GREATEST proportion of sand in its mix would be a scratch coat applied to   2._____

    A. wire lath
    B. wood lath
    C. metal lath
    D. gypsum tile

3. Sweatout on a freshly plastered wall in a room is caused by   3._____

    A. lack of ventilation in the room
    B. lack of moisture in the plaster
    C. too much heat
    D. too much circulation of air in the room

4. Frozen plaster can be detected by the appearance of _____ on the surface of the plaster.   4._____

    A. white streaks
    B. yellow streaks
    C. white spots
    D. brown spots

5. Occasionally, it is required that plaster be colored. The type of colors that should be used is   5._____

    A. water colors
    B. oil colors
    C. acid dyes
    D. mineral pigments

6. Of the following, the procedure which should NOT be followed when plastering over a crack in an old plaster wall is to   6._____

    A. wet the crack
    B. retemper the fresh plaster often
    C. use unretarded plaster
    D. remove all loose material surrounding the crack

7. A common cause of map cracking of the finish coat of plaster is   7._____

    A. there is too much water in the finish coat
    B. there is too much sand in the brown coat
    C. no admixture was added to the finish coat
    D. the scratch coat is too stiff

8. Of the following, the BEST procedure to follow when shrinkage cracks appear on a gypsum brown coat is

   A. to ignore the shrinkage cracks as the finish coat will conceal them
   B. cut out and reapply the entire brown coat
   C. cut out and fill the shrinkage cracks with scratch coat mortar
   D. cover the shrinkage cracks with a thin brown coat

9. In some cases, gypsum plaster applied in hot weather remains soft, white, and chalky, particularly above openings.
   This trouble is known as

   A. fall out
   B. alligatoring
   C. dry out
   D. blow out

10. Of the following, the MOST likely cause of the appearance of blisters on a trowelled-finished Portland cement plaster coat is that the

    A. coat is not of the correct thickness
    B. air is humid
    C. surface was not trowelled gradually
    D. water used in the plaster was too cold

11. Of the following, the BEST procedure for a plasterer to follow when repairing a large crack caused by structural movement in an old plaster wall that was laid up with wood lath is to

    A. remove all loose material and wash out the affected area with a weak solution of muriatic acid before applying the new mortar
    B. remove 6 inches of plaster from each side of the crack and nail a strip of metal lath to the existing lath before applying the new mortar
    C. remove 2 feet of plaster from each side of the crack and fill in the whole area with Bond plaster
    D. replace the entire wall with gypsum board and plywood paneling

12. Of too much water has been applied to a plaster-of-Paris mix, the plasterer should

    A. add a retardant to bring the mix to the proper consistency
    B. add an accelerator to bring the mix to the proper consistency
    C. add more plaster of Paris to bring the mix to the proper consistency
    D. discard this mix and make a new mix

Questions 13-14.

DIRECTIONS: Questions 13 and 14 are to be answered SOLELY on the basis of information contained in the following paragraph.

Tools and plastering methods have changed very little over the years. Host of the changes are mere improvements of the basic tools. The tools formerly made by hand are now machine made and are RIGIDLY constructed of light, but strong, materials in contrast to the clumsy constructions of the early types. The power-driven mixers and hoisting equipment used on large plastering jobs today produce better mortars and lighten the tasks involved.

13. According to the above paragraph, present-day tools used for plastering   13._____
    A. have made plastering much more complicated than it used to be
    B. are heavier than the old-fashioned tools they replaced
    C. produce poorer results, but speed up the job
    D. are lighter and stronger than the hand-made tools of the past

14. As used in the above paragraph, the word *rigidly* means MOST NEARLY   14._____
    A. feeble   B. weakly   C. firmly   D. flexibly

Questions 15-16.

DIRECTIONS: Questions 15 and 16 are to be answered SOLELY on the basis of information
             contained in the following paragraph.

It cannot be stressed too strongly that the greatest care should be taken in handling tools. If they are handled carelessly, serious accidents may result. Many accidents can be avoided if the back of the trowel is kept clean and if the trowel is not allowed to contain too much mortar. Where there is an EXCESS of mortar, some might drop or splash into the plasterer's eyes. Any mortar which is dropped onto the hands, wrists, ankles, or underclothing should be removed immediately.

15. The MAIN point of the above paragraph is that   15._____
    A. all accidents will be avoided if tools are kept clean
    B. most accidents can be avoided by the use of protective gloves
    C. many accidents are caused by careless handling of tools
    D. trowels should be kept free of mortar at all times

16. In the above paragraph, the word *excess* means MOST NEARLY   16._____
    A. surplus   B. minor   C. scant   D. short

17. If gypsum mortar were to drop into a plasterer's eyes, he should FIRST wash it out with   17._____
    A. a baking soda solution   B. olive oil
    C. clean water   D. warm salt water

18. For the SAFEST access to a working platform, the top end of a plasterer's ladder should   18._____
    be set _____ the top of the platform.
    A. flush with
    B. a minimum of 6 inches above
    C. a minimum of 10 inches above
    D. a minimum of 17 inches above

19. While a plasterer is working in a Housing Authority apartment, the tenant offers him   19._____
    money to watch her children while she goes shopping for about a half an hour. Of the following, the BEST course of action for the plasterer to take is to
    A. politely accept the request
    B. politely refuse the request
    C. accept the request but refuse the money
    D. ignore the tenant

20. While a plasterer is working in a Housing Authority apartment, the tenant complains to him about the shoddy floor tile repair work a maintenance man did in the apartment. Of the following, the BEST course of action for the plasterer to take is to

    A. tell the tenant he is too busy to handle the complaint
    B. tell the tenant to report her complaint to the building management
    C. report the complaint to his foreman
    D. report the complaint to the building management

20.____

21. Of the following wall materials, the one on which it is MOST difficult to secure a plaster bond is

    A. cement block
    B. brick
    C. gypsum block
    D. concrete

21.____

22. To get a good paint job on a new plaster wall, one should make certain that the

    A. wall is thoroughly dry before painting
    B. base coat is much darker than the finishing coat
    C. wall has been roughened enough to make the paint stick
    D. plaster has not completely set

22.____

23. In a three-coat plaster job, the brown coat is applied

    A. *before* the scratch coat has set
    B. *immediately after* the scratch coat
    C. *after* the scratch coat has set and partially dried
    D. *after* the scratch coat has thoroughly dried out

23.____

24. Plaster which has sand as an aggregate, when compared with plaster which has a light-weight aggregate, is

    A. a better sound absorber
    B. a better insulator
    C. less likely to crack under a sharp blow
    D. cheaper

24.____

25. In the city, the building code requires that water used in plastering MUST

    A. be perfectly clear in color
    B. not have any rust in it
    C. be fit for drinking
    D. not be fluoridated

25.____

KEY (CORRECT ANSWERS)

1. A
2. D
3. A
4. C
5. D

6. B
7. B
8. C
9. C
10. C

11. B
12. C
13. D
14. C
15. C

16. A
17. C
18. D
19. B
20. B

21. D
22. A
23. C
24. D
25. C

EXAMINATION SECTION
TEST 1

DIRECTIONS: Each question or incomplete statement is followed by several suggested answers or completions. Select the one that BEST answers the question or completes the statement. *PRINT THE LETTER OF THE CORRECT ANSWER IN THE SPACE AT THE RIGHT.*

1. Of the following materials, the one which is LEAST LIKE the others in function is 1.____
   A. perlite B. vermiculite C. gypsum D. sand

2. The scratch coat is scratched 2.____
   A. four hours after it is applied
   B. before it dries out
   C. immediately after it dries out
   D. one day after it dries out

3. Three-coat plastering *usually* has a final thickness, in inches, of 3.____
   A. 3/8 B. 4/8 C. 7/8 D. 1 1/8

4. The brown coat is applied 4.____
   A. *before* the scratch coat has set
   B. *after* the scratch coat has set but before it begins to dry
   C. *after* the scratch coat has set and partially dried
   D. *after* the scratch coat has thoroughly dried out

5. The shorter arm of a steel square is known as the 5.____
   A. tongue B. body C. blade D. heel

6. One cubic foot of sand weighs approximately 100 pounds. One cubic foot of vermiculite weighs approximately _____ pound(s). 6.____
   A. 1 B. 8 C. 50 D. 75

7. When slaking a quick-slaking lime 7.____
   A. water should be added to the lime quickly
   B. water should be added to the lime slowly
   C. water should be added to the lime without hoeing
   D. the lime should be added to the water

8. When slaking lime, the mixture should 8.____
   A. be kept cool
   B. be allowed to boil violently
   C. be allowed to boil
   D. never be hoed

9. In three-coat plastering, lime is *usually* used in 9.____
   A. the finish coat only
   B. the brown coat only
   C. the scratch coat only
   D. all three coats

15

10. The *one* of the following items which would, *most likely*, be added to a gypsum mortar mix for a brown coat is

    A. an accelerator
    B. a retarder
    C. fiber
    D. hair

11. Impurities in a mortar which may seriously affect its strength, are *most likely* to enter the mortar with the

    A. mixing water
    B. sand
    C. lime
    D. gypsum

12. Air-entraining admixtures used in stucco mortars make the stucco

    A. denser
    B. less plastic
    C. more resistant to frost action
    D. a poorer insulating material

13. When mixing stucco by hand,

    A. cement and sand should be mixed before water is added
    B. sand and water should be mixed before adding cement
    C. cement and water should be mixed before adding sand
    D. cement, sand, and water should be mixed in one operation

14. In nailing gypsum board lath to studs or furring strips, the nailing should be started _____ of the board.

    A. along the top
    B. along the bottom
    C. at the center
    D. at one end

15. Insulating board lath

    A. should be moistened before installation
    B. should be moistened during installation
    C. should be moistened after installation
    D. should not be moistened

16. The BEST key for plaster mortar is provided by

    A. plain gypsum lath
    B. perforated gypsum lath
    C. insulating board lath
    D. metal lath

17. One form of metal lath comes in sheets 27" x 96".
    The number of sheets required to cover 20 square yards without overlap is

    A. 9   B. 10   C. 11   D. 12

18. Metal lath for exterior stucco is nailed to the sheathing in such a way that there is a space between the lath and the sheathing.
    The *principal* reason for creating this space is to

    A. improve insulation
    B. provide for a good plaster key
    C. allow for a thicker coat of stucco
    D. keep the wet stucco away from the sheathing

19. Of the following masonry wall materials, the *one* which would require the MOST sand per bag of plaster is

    A. soft common brick
    B. hard-burnt brick
    C. glazed tile
    D. granite

19.____

20. The thickness of a mortar coat depends *primarily* upon the

    A. amount of mortar on the trowel
    B. pressure applied to the trowel
    C. speed with which the trowel is moved
    D. angle between face of trowel and wall surface

20.____

21. Mortar should be taken from the hawk

    A. starting at the side nearest the plasterer and working across the hawk
    B. starting at the side farthest from the plasterer and working toward the plaster
    C. at the edge farthest from the plasterer and rotating the hawk so that the last of the plaster is in the middle of the hawk
    D. at the center and then working out to the edges rotating the hawk

21.____

22. Filling in of hollow spots is done

    A. *before* the second darbying
    B. *after* the first darbying
    C. *after* troweling
    D. *after* cutting angles

22.____

23. Screeds used in plastering are made of

    A. wood   B. metal   C. plaster   D. stone

23.____

24. A plasterer would, *most likely,* use a plumb bob in connection with

    A. a darby
    B. a screed
    C. filling in
    D. cutting angles

24.____

25. A water level would *most likely* be used by a plasterer to establish a

    A. level ceiling
    B. plumb wall
    C. flat wall
    D. plumb corner

25.____

26. The soffit of a beam is the

    A. span   B. side   C. bottom   D. top

26.____

27. When colored lime plaster is required, the coloring material would be

    A. colors in oil
    B. mineral colors
    C. water colors
    D. tempera colors

27.____

28. A gypsum browning coat *usually* consists of mortar that

    A. is poorer than that of the scratch coat
    B. is richer than that of the scratch coat
    C. is the same as that of the scratch coat
    D. contains no admixtures

28.____

29. A honey-combed pattern of fine cracks in a putty coat is, *most likely*, due to

   A. a second troweling of the putty coat
   B. the brown coat being completely dried out
   C. applying water to the putty coat after placing it
   D. lack of an accelerator in the mortar

30. Dryouts in a plastered wall can *usually* be corrected by

   A. applying dry Keene's cement
   B. additional troweling
   C. spraying with water
   D. heating the room

31. Of the following statements concerning colored plaster, the one that is NOT correct is that

   A. water troweling must be avoided
   B. scaffolding requirements are the same as for ordinary plastering
   C. the work must be done without joinings
   D. the surface produced is more porous than that of ordinary plastering

32. Rotted plaster results from

   A. freezing
   B. lack of air circulation
   C. failure to spray fresh plaster, with water
   D. too much troweling

33. A white fuzz appears on the surface of a recently plastered wall. This is evidence that the plaster

   A. was oversanded
   B. had been frozen before it set
   C. had been frozen after it set
   D. dried out too slowly

34. Oversanding of mortar can LEAST readily be detected by

   A. *spreading* the mortar with a trowel
   B. *observing* the color of the mortar
   C. *scratching* the surface of the mortar after it has hardened
   D. *observing* the texture of the mortar after it has been placed

35. Acoustic plaster is *usually*

   A. applied to a brown coat of gypsum mortar
   B. applied directly to lath
   C. heavier than ordinary plaster
   D. applied in a single coat

36. The putty coat is applied when the brown coat is

   A. partially set
   B. fully set but has not started to dry out
   C. fully set and partially dried out
   D. fully dried out

37. When a finish coat is being applied in two applications, the second application is applied 37.____

    A. immediately
    B. *after* the first application has set but *before* it has started to dry out
    C. *after* the second application is partially dried out
    D. *after* the first application is dried out

38. Flashing is, *most likely,* to be used in conjunction with 38.____

    A. two-coat plastering
    B. three-coat plastering
    C. lay-on work
    D. stucco work

39. Hod carriers' ladders differ from ordinary ladders *principally* in 39.____

    A. spacing of rungs
    B. width of rungs
    C. types of materials used
    D. thickness of materials

40. The surface of an angle float is *usually* made of 40.____

    A. wood
    B. cork
    C. aluminum
    D. sponge rubber

KEY (CORRECT ANSWERS)

1. C	11. B	21. C	31. B
2. B	12. C	22. B	32. B
3. C	13. A	23. C	33. B
4. C	14. C	24. B	34. D
5. A	15. D	25. A	35. A
6. B	16. D	26. C	36. C
7. D	17. B	27. B	37. A
8. C	18. B	28. A	38. D
9. A	19. A	29. B	39. A
10. B	20. D	30. C	40. C

TEST 2

DIRECTIONS: Each question or incomplete statement is followed by several suggested answers or completions. Select the one that BEST answers the question or completes the statement. *PRINT THE LETTER OF THE CORRECT ANSWER IN THE SPACE AT THE RIGHT.*

1. A cold-rolled channel, as compared to a hot-rolled channel, has a   1.____
   A. wider flange
   B. thicker flange
   C. greater weight for the same strength
   D. sharper angle where the flanges meet the back or web

2. Of the following statements, the *one* which is CORRECT is that grounds   2.____
   A. and screeds are never used in combination
   B. are built up from dots
   C. are seldom used on ceiling work
   D. do not serve the same purpose as screeds

3. Plaster which has sand as an aggregate, when compared with plaster which has a light-weight aggregate, is   3.____
   A. a better sound absorber
   B. a better insulator
   C. less likely to crack under a sharp blow
   D. cheaper

4. A wooden mortar box for slaking lime is lined with sheet iron. Of the following, the BIGGEST advantage of the lining is   4.____
   A. a better grade putty is produced
   B. the box is easier to clean
   C. it makes the box water-tight
   D. it prevents burning of the wood

5. Keene's cement is *most nearly* like   5.____
   A. plaster of paris   B. portland cement
   C. hydrated lime   D. quicklime

6. Mortar for a scratch coat consists of 2 parts of sand and 1 part of plaster of paris. The BEST proportion for the brown coat to be applied over this scratch coat would be _____ parts sand to 1 part plaster of paris: 6.____
   A. 2   B. 2 1/2   C. 3 1/2   D. 4

7. Of the following materials, the *one* which can be re-tempered is   7.____
   A. plaster of paris   B. portland cement
   C. dehydrated lime   D. Keene's cement

21

8. Lime mortar for a base coat is *usually* compacted with a wooden float _____ it is applied.

   A. immediately after
   B. an hour after
   C. the day after
   D. as

9. Of the following statements, the *one* which is CORRECT is that

   A. a wall of vitrified brick must be furred before plastering
   B. gypsum furring tile should be wet before plastering
   C. protruding mortar joints in a brick wall should not be cut back before applying plaster to the brick
   D. a concrete wall poured in planed forms needs no preparation before plastering

10. Gypsum mortar which has set before it could be applied to a wall

    A. can be used as an accelerator when broken into powder
    B. can be retempered
    C. cannot be used for any purpose
    D. should be re-worked vigorously and then used

11. Shrinkage cracks in a putty-coat finish *most probably* indicate that troweling was

    A. started too soon
    B. continued too long
    C. continued until the plaster set
    D. insufficient

12. Metal lath for exterior use should be

    A. galvanized
    B. painted
    C. painted or galvanized
    D. bonderized

13. Metal lath should be lapped on abutting edges *at least* inch(es)

    A. 1/2   B. 1   C. 2 1/2   D. 4

14. It is unlawful to

    A. use wooden lath
    B. have ceiling lath run in one direction only
    C. break joints when using wood lath
    D. run wood lath through from room to room

15. Wane is a defect found in

    A. wood lath
    B. metal lath
    C. lime plaster
    D. gypsum plaster

16. When using metal lath on a ceiling which finishes against a masonry wall, the lath should be

    A. butted and securely fastened to the wall
    B. cut off just short of the wall
    C. bent double where it touches the wall
    D. extended at least three inches on the face of the wall and securely fastened

17. A wooden gauge is used to   17.____

    A. measure distances
    B. lay off a fixed distance
    C. measure wire diameter
    D. mix plaster

18. A mortar containing lightweight aggregate is gummy and difficult to spread.   18.____
    The plasterer *should add*

    A. less of the lightweight aggregate
    B. more gypsum
    C. some sand
    D. an accelerator

19. A beam strip would be used   19.____

    A. to clean a steel beam before plastering
    B. to remove excess material after plastering a beam
    C. as a guide to plastering the edges and bottom of a beam
    D. as a support for wet plaster on the underside of a beam

20. "Doubling up" is frequently done in applying   20.____

    A. a two-coat plaster
    B. stucco
    C. scagliola work
    D. permastone

21. The price of metal lath is $39.50 per 100 square yards. The cost of 527 square   21.____
    yards of this lath is, most nearly,

    A. $207.65   B. $207.91   C. $208.17   D. $208.43

22. The total cost of applying 221 square yards of plaster board is $343.00.   22.____
    The cost per square yard is, most nearly,

    A. $1.40   B. $1.45   C. $1.50   D. $1.55

23. In a three-coat plaster job, the scratch coat is 1/8 in. thick in front of the lath,   23.____
    the brown coat is 3/16 in. thick, and the finish coat is 1/8 in. thick.
    The total thickness of this plaster job, measured from the face of the lath, is:

    A. 7/16"   B. 1/2"   C. 9/16"   D. 5/8"

The sketches of tools shown on the following page relate to questions numbered 24 to 34 inclusive.

For each question, select the tool whose MAIN USE is indicated in the question.

24. The tool used to form and shape miter joints in cornice work is numbered: 24.____
    A. 14 B. 11 C. 4 D. 1

25. The tool used to straighten and square the angle at an inside corner is numbered: 25.____
    A. 1 B. 5 C. 7 D. 12

26. The tool used to apply plaster behind pipes and other similarly positioned objects is numbered: 26.____
    A. 2 B. 4 C. 10 D. 11

27. The tool used in producing a textured surface is numbered: 27.____
    A. 10 B. 9 C. 8 D. 6

28. The tool used for modeling in ornamental work is numbered: 28.____
    A. 11 B. 12 C. 13 D. 1.4

29. The tool used to scratch the first coat of plaster is numbered: 29.____
    A. 2 B. 5 C. 11 D. 13

30. The tool used to cut joints or grooves into plaster is numbered: 30.____
    A. 14 B. 11 C. 5 D. 2

31. The tool used to hold and carry plaster is numbered: 31.____
    A. 6 B. 8 C. 9 D. 10

32. The tool used to clean out and to finish an inside corner after it has been floated is numbered: 32.____
    A. 2 B. 6 C. 8 D. 10

33. The tool used for pointing is numbered: 33.____
    A. 3 B. 4 C. 5 D. 11

34. The tool used in determining whether or not a wall is plumb is numbered: 34.____
    A. 1 B. 2 C. 7 D. 12

5 (#2)

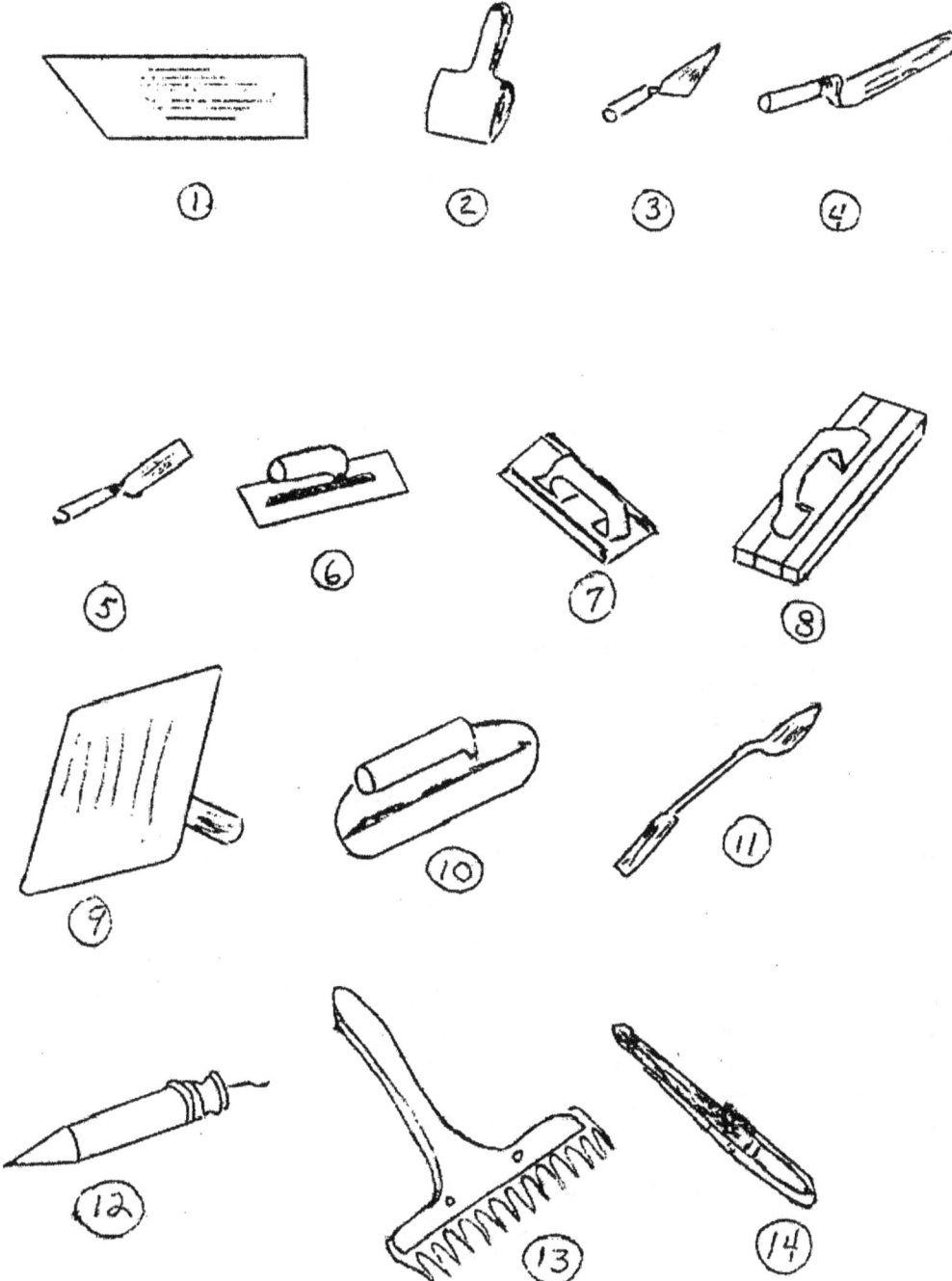

35. The tool that is not shown on the sketch page is a(n):

    A. Hawk
    B. Joint Former
    C. Float
    D. Joint Rod

36. When *estimating* materials for interior plaster, *consideration* must be given to the number of coats. *Estimating,* as used in the sentence, means

    A. calculating approximately
    B. purchasing
    C. mixing together
    D. finishing

37. *Consideration,* as used in the sentence in question 36, means

    A. extra weight
    B. careful thought
    C. firmness
    D. additions

38. When *computing* quantities of plaster for the scratch coat, no *allowance* may be made for the space occupied by the metal lath.
    Computing, as used in the sentence, means

    A. figuring
    B. preparing
    C. slaking
    D. packing

39. *Allowance,* as used in the sentence in question 38, means

    A. deduction
    B. addition
    C. leeway
    D. closing

40. In general, in work such as scratch and brown coats, each plasterer will require one helper to keep the plasterer supplied with materials. In special work, such as finish work, paneling, and molding, the number of helpers needed will vary from 1/3 to 2/3 the number of plasterers.
    According to the paragraph above,

    A. the scratch coat is more difficult to apply than the finish coat
    B. the cost of paneling is less than that of applying a brown coat
    C. the length of time required to complete molding work can be shortened by supplying more helpers
    D. more helpers are required per plasterer for a brown coat than for a finish coat

KEY (CORRECT ANSWERS)

1. A
2. C
3. D
4. B
5. A

6. B
7. D
8. C
9. A
10. A

11. D
12. A
13. B
14. D
15. A

16. D
17. B
18. C
19. C
20. A

21. C
22. D
23. A
24. D
25. C

26. B
27. A
28. A
29. D
30. A

31. C
32. A
33. A
34. D
35. B

36. A
37. B
38. A
39. A
40. D

EXAMINATION SECTION
TEST 1

DIRECTIONS: Each question or incomplete statement is followed by several suggested answers or completions. Select the one that BEST answers the question or completes the statement. *PRINT THE LETTER OF THE CORRECT ANSWER IN THE SPACE AT THE RIGHT.*

1. Plastering has just been completed in a room.
   The PROPER way to ventilate the room to dry out the plaster when the outside weather conditions are moderate is to

   A. keep the window shut
   B. open the bottom window all the way
   C. open the top and bottom window 2 inches
   D. open the top window all the way

   1.____

2. A coat of plaster which is scratched deliberately would MOST likely be

   A. used in two-coat work only
   B. the first coat placed
   C. the second coat placed
   D. condemned by the inspector

   2.____

3. Screeds in plaster work are used to

   A. remove larger sizes of sand
   B. hold the batch of plaster before it is applied
   C. apply the plaster to the wall
   D. guide the plasterer in making an even wall

   3.____

4. The FIRST coat of plaster over rock lath should be a _____ plaster.

   A. gypsum   B. lime
   C. portland cement   D. puzzolan cement

   4.____

5. In plastering, a *hawk* is used to _____ plaster.

   A. apply   B. hold   C. scratch   D. smooth

   5.____

6. Where bond plaster is specified for the scratch coat, it is GENERALLY required that the bond plaster be

   A. mixed with lime putty
   B. mixed neat without the addition of sand
   C. slaked at least 24 hours before use
   D. mixed with gypsum gaging plaster

   6.____

7. For the finish coat of a three-coat plaster job, it is MOST likely that the specifications would call for

   A. vermiculite   B. silicon
   C. perlite   D. gypsum

   7.____

29

8. In three-coat plaster, the finish coat follows the brown coat. The minimum number of days that must elapse after the brown coat is completed before the finish coat may be applied is MOST NEARLY

   A. 1   B. 3   C. 17   D. 32

9. Mortar for the white or finishing coat of a three-coat plaster job consists USUALLY of a mixture of

   A. slaked lime, water, and sand
   B. slaked lime, water, sand, and plaster of paris
   C. gypsum cement, water, sand, and plaster of paris
   D. slaked lime, water, and plaster of paris

10. The ADVANTAGES of gypsum mortar over lime mortar for use in plaster work are that gypsum mortar is stronger and _____ than lime mortar.

    A. is more compact
    B. sets more quickly
    C. works more easily
    D. contains more entrained air

11. Before quicklime can be used for plaster, it must be

    A. slaked   B. burned   C. floated   D. glazed

12. When a hard plaster is required, as in halls, the one of the following that would MOST likely be used is

    A. lime
    C. stucco
    B. Keene's cement
    D. marbling

13. To give plaster a hard finish, hydrated lime is mixed with

    A. white cement
    C. white lead
    B. linseed oil putty
    D. plaster of paris

14. The purpose of a ground in plaster work is to

    A. provide a key for the plaster
    B. help the plasterer make an even wall
    C. prevent the plasterer's scaffold from slipping
    D. hold the loose plaster before it is placed

15. When a lightweight plaster is required, the one of the following fine aggregates that is MOST likely to be used is

    A. cinders
    C. talc
    B. sand
    D. vermiculite

16. Of the following fireproofing materials, the one which would be MOST frequently used to fireproof steel columns in a fireproof building is

    A. sheet rock
    C. brick
    B. vermiculite plaster
    D. rock lath

17. The one of the following items that is LEAST related to the others is 17._____

    A. rock wool   B. wall board
    C. sheet rock   D. rock lath

18. The first layer of plaster placed in a three-coat plaster job is called the _____ coat. 18._____

    A. brown   B. scratch   C. hard   D. white

19. The practice of applying the brown coat to a wall on the day after the scratch coat of gypsum plaster was applied is GENERALLY considered 19._____

    A. *satisfactory*
    B. *satisfactory* only if the temperature is between 50° and 70° F
    C. *unsatisfactory* because 7 days must elapse between the application of the scratch and brown coats
    D. *unsatisfactory* because at least 3 days must elapse between the application of the scratch and brown coats

20. A three-coat plaster job is to be 7/8 inches thick. Of the following, the thickness of the individual coats, in inches, would be MOST NEARLY scratch _____, brown _____, finish 20._____

    A. 1/8; 1/2; 1/4   B. 3/8; 3/8; 1/8
    C. 11/16; 1/8, 1/16   D. 5/16; 1/4; 5/16

21. The quantity of water USUALLY required for the scratch coat of a 1:3 lime plaster is 21._____

    A. 5 1/2 gallons water per cubic foot
    B. 0.60 by weight
    C. sufficient water to make a workable mix
    D. sufficient water to give a 3-inch slump

22. Of the following, the plasterer's tool USUALLY used to force plaster into the lath is a 22._____

    A. trowel   B. screed   C. darby   D. hawk

23. If to calcined gypsum is added about one-sixth of its weight of hydrated lime to improve its plasticity and enough retarder to make it set in about two hours, the product is USUALLY known as 23._____

    A. Keene's cement   B. gypsum neat plaster
    C. plaster of paris   D. gaging plaster

24. The thickness of three-coat plaster on metal lath is USUALLY 24._____

    A. 1 1/2"   B. 7/8"   C. 1 1/8"   D. 1 1/2"

25. A large crack in a plaster wall appears two years after completion of the building. The crack starts from the corner of a door and extends diagonally to the edge of the wall. The cause of this crack is PROBABLY due to 25._____

    A. improper application of the scratch coat
    B. precipitation of the lime in the plaster
    C. improper tying of the lath to the furring
    D. settlement of the building

26. In the application of plaster on a wall that is to be painted, an inspector should see that
    A. the scratch coat shall not completely cover the lath so that the brown coat may be bonded to both the scratch coat and the lath
    B. the brown coat is not applied until the scratch coat is thoroughly dry
    C. the finish coat is not applied until the brown coat is thoroughly dry
    D. no plastering is done when the temperature in the room is less than 70° F

27. When plastering a wall surface of glazed tile, it is MOST important that the tile be
    A. wet   B. dry   C. scored   D. raked

28. In plastering, coves would MOST likely be found where the wall meets
    A. ceiling   B. wall   C. floor   D. column

29. When using tape to conceal joints in dry wall construction, the FIRST operation is
    A. channelling the grooves between boards
    B. applying cement to the joints
    C. sanding the edges of the joints
    D. packing the tape into the joints

30. For the FIRST coat of plaster on wire lath, plaster of paris is mixed with
    A. cement   B. sand   C. lime   D. mortar

KEY (CORRECT ANSWERS)

1.	C	16.	B
2.	B	17.	A
3.	D	18.	B
4.	A	19.	A
5.	B	20.	B
6.	B	21.	C
7.	D	22.	A
8.	B	23.	B
9.	D	24.	B
10.	B	25.	D
11.	A	26.	C
12.	B	27.	C
13.	D	28.	A
14.	B	29.	B
15.	D	30.	B

TEST 2

DIRECTIONS: Each question or incomplete statement is followed by several suggested answers or completions. Select the one that BEST answers the question or completes the statement. *PRINT THE LETTER OF THE CORRECT ANSWER IN THE SPACE AT THE RIGHT.*

1. Lightweight plaster would be made with

    A. sand
    B. cinders
    C. potash
    D. vermiculite

    1._____

2. The SECOND coat of plaster to be applied on a three-coat plaster job is the _____ coat.

    A. brown B. scratch C. white D. keene

    2._____

3. The FIRST coat of plaster over rock lath should be a _____ plaster.

    A. gypsum
    B. lime
    C. portland cement
    D. pozzolan cement

    3._____

4. When nailing gypsum board lath to studs or furring strips, the nailing should be started _____ of the board.

    A. along the top
    B. along the bottom
    C. at the center
    D. at one end

    4._____

5. A wooden mortar box for slaking lime is lined with sheet iron.
   Of the following, the GREATEST advantage of the lining is that

    A. a better grade putty is produced
    B. the box is easier to clean
    C. it makes the box water-tight
    D. it prevents burning of the wood

    5._____

6. The Building Code requires that water used in plastering MUST

    A. be perfectly clear in color
    B. not have any rust in it
    C. be fit for drinking
    D. not be fluoridated

    6._____

7. The purpose of scratching the surface of the first coat of patching stucco is to

    A. spread the patching stucco over a wide area
    B. give the surface a textured finish
    C. provide a gripping surface for the next coat of patching stucco
    D. press the patching stucco into the hole to be repaired

    7._____

8. When filling in large cracks and holes up to 2 inches in diameter in plaster walls, it is BEST to use

    A. spackle
    B. patching plaster
    C. gypsum wallboard
    D. tile

    8._____

9. It is DESIRABLE for a putty knife used for patching plaster cracks to be flexible because a flexible putty knife 9.____

   A. makes it difficult for the user to cut his hands while applying the plaster
   B. is easier to keep clean than one made of rigid material
   C. can press the patching materials into the crack, filling it completely
   D. makes it possible to pick up the exact amount of plaster required

10. Plaster which has sand as an aggregate, when compared with plaster which has a lightweight aggregate, is 10.____

    A. a better sound absorber
    B. a better insulator
    C. less likely to crack under a sharp blow
    D. cheaper

11. Of the following, the one that may MOST likely be the cause of map cracking in the finish coat of plaster is 11.____

    A. a weak brown coat
    B. too much moisture present
    C. a warm dry draft blowing on fresh plaster
    D. too much retarder in the mix

12. An inspector reports a dryout in the room that has just been plastered. The MOST appropriate course of action to take is to 12.____

    A. wait until the plaster sets and determine the extent of the damage
    B. order the dryout removed and replastered
    C. order an increase in the amount of retarder used in the mix
    D. allow the contractor to spray water on the dry spot so that setting action may start again

13. The temperature below which it is NOT good practice to do plastering in is, in degrees F, MOST NEARLY 13.____

    A. 72   B. 65   C. 50   D. 36

14. Gaging plaster that is used to accelerate the setting time of finish coat plaster is GENERALLY 14.____

    A. plaster of paris   B. hydrated lime
    C. keene's cement   D. dolomitic lime

15. Quicklime used in preparing plaster is lime that 15.____

    A. gives a harder finish than hydrated lime
    B. must be slaked before using
    C. sets faster than hydrated lime
    D. need not be slaked before using

16. Of the following, the one that is SOMETIMES mixed into plaster to increase the strength is 16.____

    A. hair   B. paint   C. shellac   D. glue

17. The finish coat of plaster should be trowelled after it begins to harden because　　　　17.____

    A. this will give a harder surface
    B. it will bond better with the brown coat
    C. this will result in a stronger plaster
    D. most of the shrinkage would have taken place and cracks can be filled

18. Acoustic plaster is used where it is desired to provide　　　　18.____

    A. soundproofing　　　　　　　　　B. fireproofing
    C. a lightweight structure　　　　　D. a vermin-proof structure

19. Keene's cement plaster is used　　　　19.____

    A. where the plaster is not to be painted
    B. where a hard surface is desired
    C. where there is no scratch coat
    D. on perforated rock lath

20. One form of metal lath comes in sheets 27" x 96".　　　　20.____
    The number of sheets required to cover 20 square yards without overlap is

    A. 9　　　　B. 10　　　　C. 11　　　　D. 12

21. Dry plaster will absorb water from the patching material, weakening and shrinking it.　　　　21.____
    Based on the information in this statement, it would be ADVISABLE to take which one
    of the following actions in the process of patching a plaster crack?

    A. Mix the plaster with a lot of extra water
    B. Apply water-eased paint to the wall immediately
    C. Apply plaster powder to the crack, then pour water in over it
    D. Dampen the area surrounding the patch with a sponge

22. Vermiculite is used in plaster to　　　　22.____

    A. reduce weight
    B. permit easier cleaning
    C. give architectural effects
    D. reduce the mixing water required

23. The volume, in cubic feet, of a room 8'6" wide by 10'6" long by 8'8" high is MOST　　　　23.____
    NEARLY

    A. 770　　　　B. 774　　　　C. 778　　　　D. 782

24. Assume that from a study of your inventory control card for patching plaster you find that　　　　24.____
    you are issuing 5 one-pound bags per day. Agency policy requires that you maintain a
    reserve supply for five days supply on hand at all times.
    If it takes twenty work days to have a requisition for this item filled, you should submit a
    requisition for additional supplies when your balance on hand is

    A. 25　　　　B. 75　　　　C. 100　　　　D. 125

25. Gypsum lath for plastering is purchased in　　　　25.____

    A. strips 5/16" x 1 1/2" x 4'　　　　B. rolls 3/8" x 48" x 96"
    C. boards 1/2" x 16" x 48"　　　　D. sheets 5/16" x 27" x 96"

KEY (CORRECT ANSWERS)

1.	D	11.	A
2.	A	12.	D
3.	A	13.	C
4.	C	14.	A
5.	B	15.	B
6.	C	16.	A
7.	C	17.	D
8.	B	18.	A
9.	C	19.	B
10.	D	20.	B

21. D
22. A
23. B
24. D
25. C

EXAMINATION SECTION
TEST 1

DIRECTIONS: Each question or incomplete statement is followed by several suggested answers or completions. Select the one that BEST answers the question or completes the statement. *PRINT THE LETTER OF THE CORRECT ANSWER IN THE SPACE AT THE RIGHT.*

Questions 1-5.

DIRECTIONS: For Questions 1 through 5, inclusive, Column I lists frequently used construction terms. Column II lists some of the building trades. For each item listed in Column I, enter in the appropriate space at the right the capital letter in front of the trade listed in Column II that is MOST closely associated with the item. Each trade may be used more than once or not at all.

COLUMN I	COLUMN II	
1. Bed	A. Plumbing	1.____
2. Wiping	B. Plastering	2.____
3. Brown	C. Carpentry	3.____
4. Key	D. Masonry	4.____
5. Bridging	E. Painting	5.____
	F. Steelwork	
	G. Roofing	

6. A *cricket* would be found

    A. on a roof
    B. at a structural steel connection
    C. supporting reinforcing steel
    D. over a window

6.____

7. *Cutting in* is done when

    A. trimming a stud to size
    B. fitting a bat in a brick wall
    C. painting in tight corners
    D. trimming tallow for a wiped joint

7.____

8. *Corbeling* results in

    A. strengthening a concrete column
    B. waterproofing a foundation wall
    C. anchoring a steel girder to a bearing wall
    D. increasing the thickness of a brick wall

8.____

9. Solder used for copper gutters is MOST frequently

   A. 30-70   B. 40-60   C. 50-50   D. 60-40

10. A jack rafter runs from

    A. plate to ridge
    B. hip to ridge
    C. plate to hip
    D. plate to plate

11. The one of the following items that is LEAST related to the others is

    A. sill   B. joist   C. sole   D. newel

12. A *fire cut* is made on

    A. timber posts
    B. rafters
    C. floor joists
    D. lathing

13. The one of the following items that is LEAST related to the others is

    A. joist hanger
    B. pintle
    C. bridle iron
    D. stirrup

14. The PROPER order of nailing sub-flooring and bridging is

    A. top of bridging, bottom of bridging, sub-flooring
    B. bottom of bridging, sub-flooring, top of bridging
    C. top of bridging, sub-flooring, bottom of bridging
    D. bottom of bridging, top of bridging, sub-flooring

15. Sleepers would be found in

    A. walls   B. doors   C. footings   D. floors

16. The one of the following woods that is MOST commonly used for finish flooring is

    A. hemlock   B. cypress   C. larch   D. oak

17. Spacing of studs in a stud partition is MOST frequently _____" o.c.

    A. 12   B. 14   C. 16   D. 18

18. A hollow masonry wall should be used in preference to a solid masonry wall when the characteristic MOST desired is

    A. insulation
    B. strength
    C. beauty
    D. durability

19. The arrangement of headers and stretchers in brickwork is known as the

    A. bond   B. stringer   C. lacing   D. stile

20. Of the following, the reason that is LEAST likely to justify pointing brickwork is that pointing _____ the wall.

    A. improves the appearance of
    B. helps prevent cracking of
    C. increases the useful life of
    D. helps waterproof

21. The purpose of flashing is to

    A. keep water out
    B. speed the set of mortar
    C. anchor a cornice
    D. cover exposed joists

22. The one of the following classes of wall that would LEAST likely be the outside wall of a building is a

    A. spandrel   B. fire   C. curtain   D. parapet

23. Lime is added to mortar USUALLY to

    A. increase the strength of the mortar
    B. make the mortar water resistant
    C. make it easier to apply the mortar
    D. improve the appearance of the mortar joint

24. Efflorescence on the face of a brick wall is BEST removed by scrubbing with a solution of

    A. muriatic acid
    B. sodium silicate
    C. oxalic acid
    D. calcium oxide

25. The one of the following that is NOT a defect in painting is

    A. chalking
    B. checking
    C. alligatoring
    D. waning

26. The one of the following ingredients of a paint that would be called the *vehicle* is

    A. white lead
    B. turpentine
    C. linseed oil
    D. pigment

27. The one of the following that is used as a rust preventative in the prime coat for painting steel is

    A. aluminum
    B. red lead
    C. titanium dioxide
    D. carbon black

28. *Boxing*, with reference to paint, means

    A. thinning   B. mixing   C. spreading   D. drying

29. When painting new wood, filling of nail holes and cracks with putty should be done

    A. 24 hours before priming
    B. immediately before priming
    C. after priming and before the second coat
    D. after the second coat and before the finish coat

30. The one of the following that is the size of a reinforcing rod MOST commonly used in reinforced concrete construction is

    A. 1 3/4" ϕ B. 18 gauge   C. #9   D. 2 ST3

31. Honeycombing in concrete is USUALLY caused by

    A. too plastic a mix
    B. high fall of concrete
    C. mixing too long
    D. inadequate vibration

32. A concrete mix is indicated as 1:2:3 1/2 mix. The number 2 refers to the proportion by volume of

    A. water B. cement C. gravel D. sand

33. Specifications for concrete mixes frequently call for the use of dry sand. The reason for this is that the additional water in wet sand will

    A. make it more difficult to place the concrete
    B. decrease the strength of the concrete
    C. cause the sand and stone to segregate
    D. increase the cost of waterproofing

34. Curing of concrete serves PRIMARILY to

    A. prevent freezing of the concrete
    B. permit early removal of forms
    C. delay setting of the concrete
    D. prevent evaporation of moisture

35. The MAIN reason that forms for concrete work are oiled is to

    A. *permit* easy removal of forms
    B. *prevent* rust marks on the concrete
    C. *prevent* bleeding of water
    D. *permit* easier vibration of the concrete

36. The one of the following terms that is LEAST related to the others is

    A. 5-ply B. mastic
    C. vapor barrier D. flashing

37. Before quicklime can be used for plaster, it must be

    A. slaked B. burned C. floated D. glazed

38. When a hard plaster is required, as in halls, the one of the following that would MOST likely be used is

    A. lime B. Keene's cement
    C. stucco D. marbling

39. To give plaster a hard finish, hydrated lime is mixed with

    A. white cement B. linseed oil putty
    C. white lead D. plaster of paris

40. The purpose of a ground in plaster work is to

    A. provide a key for the plaster
    B. help the plasterer make an even wall
    C. prevent the plasterer's scaffold from slipping
    D. hold the loose plaster before it is placed

41. When a lightweight plaster is required, the one of the following fine aggregates that is MOST likely to be used is

    A. cinders
    B. sand
    C. talc
    D. vermiculite

42. Of the following fireproofing materials, the one which would be MOST frequently used to fireproof steel columns in a fireproof building is

    A. sheet rock
    B. vermiculite plaster
    C. brick
    D. rock lath

43. The one of the following items that is LEAST related to the others is

    A. rock wool
    B. wall board
    C. sheet rock
    D. rock lath

44. The first layer of plaster placed in a 3-coat plaster job is called the _____ coat.

    A. brown   B. scratch   C. hard   D. white

45. The one of the following symbols that represents a steel section which is MOST similar in appearance to a W section is

    A. U   B. L   C. I   D. Z

46. A plate used to connect two steel angles in a roof truss is known as a(n)

    A. angle iron
    B. gusset plate
    C. bearing plate
    D. tie bar

47. Steel beams are COMMONLY anchored to brick walls by

    A. government anchors
    B. tie rods
    C. eye bars
    D. anchor bolts

48. Rivet holes are lined up with a

    A. set screw
    B. ginnywink
    C. drift pin
    D. trivet

49. A sewer that carries BOTH storm water and sewage is called a _____ sewer.

    A. sanitary   B. flush   C. combined   D. mixed

50. A fresh air inlet for a house drainage system would be connected to the system

    A. just ahead of the house trap
    B. at each horizontal branch line
    C. at the top of the stack through the roof
    D. at the trap of each water closet

KEY (CORRECT ANSWERS)

1. D	11. D	21. A	31. D	41. D
2. A	12. C	22. B	32. D	42. B
3. B	13. B	23. C	33. B	43. A
4. B	14. C	24. A	34. D	44. B
5. C	15. D	25. D	35. A	45. C
6. A	16. D	26. C	36. C	46. B
7. C	17. C	27. B	37. A	47. A
8. D	18. A	28. B	38. B	48. C
9. C	19. A	29. C	39. D	49. C
10. C	20. B	30. C	40. B	50. A

TEST 2

DIRECTIONS: Each question or incomplete statement is followed by several suggested answers or completions. Select the one that BEST answers the question or completes the statement. *PRINT THE LETTER OF THE CORRECT ANSWER IN THE SPACE AT THE RIGHT.*

Questions 1-5.

DIRECTIONS: Column I consists of a list of trades, and Column II lists tools used in those trades. In the space at the right, opposite the number of the trade in Column I, write the letter preceding the tool of the trade in Column II.

COLUMN I		COLUMN II	
1. Carpenter	A.	Mop	1.____
2. Plumber	B.	Hawk	2.____
3. Plasterer	C.	Miter box	3.____
4. Bricklayer	D.	Shave-hook	4.____
5. Roofer	E.	Jointing tool	5.____

Questions 6-7.

DIRECTIONS: Questions 6 and 7 refer to the mortar joints shown below.

6. The mortar joint MOST frequently used on common brickwork is 6.____
   A. 1   B. 2   C. 3   D. 4

7. The mortar joint which would NOT usually be made unless an outside scaffold was used is 7.____
   A. 1   B. 2   C. 3   D. 4

8. A rectangular yard is 50'0" long by 8'6" wide. 8.____
   The area of the yard is, in square feet,
   A. 420.0   B. 422.5   C. 425.0   D. 427.5

9. A rectangular court is 23'0" long by 9'6" wide. 9.___
   The length of the diagonal is MOST NEARLY

   A. 24'8"   B. 24'10"   C. 25'2"   D. 25'6"

10. Concrete weighs 150 pounds per cubic foot. 10.___
    A slab of concrete 6'0" long by 3'6" wide by 1'4" thick weighs MOST NEARLY _____ pounds.

    A. 4150   B. 4200   C. 4250   D. 4300

11. A building 32'0" by 65'0" occupies a lot 60'0" by 110'0". The ratio of building area to lot 11.___
    area is MOST NEARLY

    A. 0.32   B. 0.33   C. 0.34   D. 0.35

12. When painting wood, puttying of nail holes and cracks is done 12.___

    A. before any painting is started
    B. after the priming coat is applied
    C. after the finish coat is applied
    D. at any stage in the painting

13. The process of pouring paint from one container to another in order to mix it is known as 13.___

    A. bleeding   B. boxing   C. cutting   D. stirring

14. Paint is *thinned* with 14.___

    A. linseed oil   B. turpentine
    C. varnish   D. gasoline

15. A wood screw which can be tightened by a wrench is known as a _____ screw. 15.___

    A. lag   B. Philips   C. carriage   D. monkey

16. To permit easy removal of forms from concrete, the inside surfaces of the forms are often 16.___
    coated with

    A. paint   B. oil   C. water   D. asphalt

17. Sixteen pieces of 2 x 4 lumber, each 10'6" long, contain a total of _____ FBM. 17.___

    A. 110   B. 111   C. 112   D. 113

18. The consistency of concrete is measured with a 18.___

    A. Vicat needle   B. slump cone
    C. hook gage   D. bourdon gage

19. End-matched lumber would MOST likely be used for 19.___

    A. sheathing   B. roofing   C. flooring   D. siding

20. A post or shore is to be placed midway between columns to support the formwork for a 20.___
    reinforced concrete girder. The post should be cut

    A. short, so that wedging is required
    B. to exact length

C. long, so that it will have to be driven into place
D. in two pieces, to permit jackknifing into place

21. Batter boards are set by a

    A. mason   B. plumber   C. roofer   D. surveyor

22. Of the following terms, all of which refer to tools, the one which is LEAST related to the others is

    A. back   B. box-end   C. cross-cut   D. rip

23. Of the following tools, the one which is LEAST like the others is

    A. brace and bit   B. draw-knife
    C. plans   D. spoke-shave

24. When wood splits easily, it is advisable to drill a hole for each nail. The hole for the nail should be _____ the nail.

    A. larger in diameter than
    B. smaller in diameter than
    C. exactly the same diameter as
    D. less than one-quarter the length of

25. The length of a 10-penny nail, in inches, is

    A. $2\frac{1}{2}$ B. 3   C. $3\frac{1}{2}$ D. 4

26. The decimal equivalent of 31/64 of an inch is MOST NEARLY

    A. 0.45   B. 0.46   C. 0.47   D. 0.48

27. Of the following, the one which is BEST classified as an abrasive is

    A. a saw   B. a chisel   C. graphite   D. sandpaper

28. Of the following construction materials, the one which would MOST likely be stored directly on the ground is

    A. brick   B. cement   C. steel   D. wood

29. The strength of brick walls is based upon the type of mortar used. The relative strength of the various types of mortar, in descending order, is

    A. cement, lime, cement-lime
    B. lime, cement-lime, cement
    C. cement-lime, cement, lime
    D. cement, cement-lime, lime

30. Coating reinforcing rods with oil before placing them in the forms is

    A. *good* practice, because it prevents rusting
    B. *poor* practice, because it makes the rods difficult to handle
    C. *good* practice if the forms are oiled
    D. *poor* practice, because it destroys the bond between the concrete and the rods

31. If the mixing plant should break down after one-half the concrete has been mixed for a floor, the BEST thing to do would be to

   A. take the concrete out of the forms and throw it away
   B. spread the available concrete evenly over the floor area
   C. block off one-half of the floor area and place the available concrete in the blocked-off area
   D. keep mixing the concrete in the forms with shovels until the plant is repaired

32. Splicing of reinforcing bars is accomplished by

   A. using wire ties
   B. underlapping the bars
   C. hooking the bars
   D. using metal clips

33. A sanitary sewer carries

   A. storm water only
   B. sewage only
   C. sewage and storm water
   D. the discharge from a sewage plant

34. A neat line

   A. is the result of good workmanship
   B. is used in concrete construction only
   C. defines an outer limit of a structure
   D. defines an outer limit of excavation for a structure

35. Continued trowelling of a cement-finish floor for a building is

   A. *good* practice, because it provides a smooth floor
   B. *poor* practice, because it produces a slippery floor
   C. *poor* practice, because it brings the fines to the surface
   D. *good* practice, because it insures proper mixing of the cement finish

36. In reinforced concrete form work, a beveled chamfer strip is used to

   A. reinforce the outside of the forms
   B. reinforce the inside of the forms
   C. seal leaks in the forms
   D. do none of the foregoing

37. Cracks in lumber due to contraction along annual rings are known as

   A. checks
   B. wanes
   C. pitch pockets
   D. dry rot

38. Honeycombing is MOST likely to occur in construction involving

   A. steel   B. concrete   C. wood   D. masonry

39. Floor beams are sometimes crowned to

   A. provide arch action
   B. eliminate deflection
   C. strengthen the floor
   D. provide a more nearly level floor than would be provided by straight beams

40. In brickwork, a rowlock course consists of

   A. headers
   B. stretchers
   C. bricks laid on edge
   D. bricks laid so that the longest dimension is vertical

41. The term *bond,* as used in bricklaying, refers to

   A. structure only
   B. pattern only
   C. structure and pattern
   D. color and finish of individual bricks

42. Concrete is a mixture of cement,

   A. fine aggregate, coarse aggregate, and water
   B. sand, and water
   C. stone, and water
   D. sand, and stone

43. Consistency, when used in connection with concrete, refers to the

   A. seven-day strength
   B. twenty-eight day strength
   C. initial set before forms are removed
   D. plasticity of freshly mixed concrete

44. Brick may be used for the facing material in both faced walls and veneered walls. The distinction between the two types of walls relates to

   A. bonding or lack of bonding between facing and backing
   B. type of material in facing and backing
   C. relative thickness of facing and backing
   D. the type of mortar used

45. A plaster *key* is NOT formed on _____ lath.

   A. wood   B. metal
   C. expanded metal   D. gypsum

46. Of the following, the BEST tool to use to make a hole in a coping stone is a

   A. star drill   B. coping saw
   C. pneumatic grinder   D. diamond wheel dresser

47. Roughing refers to work performed by a

   A. carpenter   B. bricklayer
   C. plumber   D. roofer

48. A post supporting a handrail is known as a

   A. tread   B. riser   C. newel   D. bevel

49. The live load on a floor is 40 pounds per square foot. The floor joists are on a 14'0" span and are spaced 2'6" on centers.
The maximum live load carried by a joist, in pounds, is MOST NEARLY

    A. 700   B. 933   C. 1167   D. 1400

50. Of the following terms, the one LEAST related to the others is

    A. ground   B. purlin
    C. rafter   D. ridge board

KEY (CORRECT ANSWERS)

1. C	11. A	21. D	31. C	41. C
2. D	12. B	22. B	32. A	42. A
3. B	13. B	23. A	33. B	43. D
4. E	14. B	24. B	34. C	44. A
5. A	15. A	25. B	35. C	45. D
6. C	16. B	26. D	36. D	46. A
7. A	17. C	27. D	37. A	47. C
8. C	18. B	28. A	38. B	48. C
9. B	19. C	29. D	39. D	49. D
10. B	20. A	30. D	40. C	50. A

EXAMINATION SECTION
TEST 1

DIRECTIONS: Answer the following questions directly, briefly, and succinctly.

1. What is the steel or aluminum plate used to hold the plaster while working called?
2. What are the coats in a three-coat job called?
3. What kind of plaster is usually used in toilet rooms?
4. Of what does lime putty consist?
5. What gauging material should be used for mouldings?
6. What three materials are usually used for a lime scratch coat?
7. What is plasterer's putty made of?
8. What tool is used on a putty coat?
9. Why do you add a retarder to the finish plaster mix?
10. What tool is used on a sand-finish coat?

KEY (CORRECT ANSWERS)

1. Hawk

2.
   1. Scratch (first) (render)
   2. Brown (rough) (second)
   3. Finish (white)

3. Keene cement

4. Finishing plaster and hydrated lime

5. Plaster of paris

6. Lime
   Sand
   Fiber (long hair)

7. Slaked lime and water

8. Trowel

9. Prevent setting too fast

10. Float

TEST 2

DIRECTIONS: Answer the following questions directly, briefly, and succinctly.

1. What tool is used for straightening out angles?
2. What is used when wood and brick join at a corner?
3. What is the usual total thickness of the scratch and brown coats applied on rock lath?
4. What gauging material should be used to imitate tile?
5. What is meant by a *cat face*?
6. What coat is the richest mix in three-coat work?
7. Name two gauging materials.
8. What is used to hold temporary grounds to the walls?
9. What is the LAST thing done to the white coat?
10. How many coats of plaster are usually applied to tile work?

KEY (CORRECT ANSWERS)

1. Mitre rod
   Feather edge
   Straight edge

2. Metal lath

3. 3/8 to 1/2 inch

4. Keene cement

5. Rough place (blemish) in white (finish) coat

6. First (scratch)

7. Keene cement
   Plaster of paris
   Portland cement
   Moulding plaster
   Calcined gypsum

8. Moulding plaster
   Nails

9. Brushed off with water

10. Two
    Three

TEST 3

DIRECTIONS: Answer the following questions directly, briefly, and succinctly.

1. How many coats of plaster are usually put over hollow tile?
2. What three tools are used for leveling off the rough plaster coat?
3. How long should hydrated lime be slaked before using?
4. In which coat is the fibre put when plastering on metal lath?
5. Why is wood lath wetted before plaster is applied?
6. What is the usual method of supporting heavy plaster castings?
7. What three common types of lath is plaster put on?
8. Why does newly finish plaster sometimes show hairline cracks?
9. Name four tools you use to make a wall true.
10. What four materials are usually used for a stucco scratch coat?

KEY (CORRECT ANSWERS)

1. Two
   Three

2. Darby
   Straight edge
   Wood float

3. At least 24 hours

4. Scratch (first)
   Brown

5. To swell lath
   To keep from buckling

6. Wadding
   Ties (wires)
   Hangers

7. Metal
   Wood
   Rock
   Fiberboard

8. Too rich a mix
   Dried too quickly
   Not troweled enough

9. Straight edge
   Darby
   Float
   Plumb bob
   Mitre rod
   Feather edge

10. Cement
    Lime
    Sand
    Fiber (long hair)

TEST 4

DIRECTIONS: Answer the following questions directly, briefly, and succinctly.

1. What is used besides small nails to hold guide strips in place?
2. What is the operation called for filling in the open joints of a run of molding?
3. What is the operation called for applying fresh plaster to the back of a mold before placing it on a wall?
4. What material is used to keep the plaster from setting too fast?
5. What is a small double-ended trowel called?
6. What is the cutting edge of the mold usually made of?
7. What tool is used to produce panelled effects in plaster work?
8. What tool is used after the mold to finish panelling?
9. What is a retarder usually made of?
10. What is used to guide the mold?
11. What is the form called that is used for cornice work?
12. What are the surfaces on which the mold rides called?
13. What is the operation called for making a plaster mold directly on a wall or ceiling?
14. What is a deeply recessed panel ceiling called?
15. What is the series called for small projecting blocks sometimes put in the bottom member of a cornice mold?

2 (#4)

KEY (CORRECT ANSWERS)

1. Dabs (knots) of plaster

2. Pointing up (mitering)

3. Buttering (sticking) (grouting) (wadding)

4. Retarder (glue)

5. Slick (small tool)

6. Sheet metal

7. Mold (templet)

8. Pointing tool
   Mitre rod
   Joint rod
   Small tool

9. Glue (bones)
   Cream of tartar (tartaric acid)

10. Guide strip (running strip) (cornice strip)
    Slipper

11. Mold (contour board) (templet)

12. Screeds (running strips)

13. Running (cornicing)

14. Coffered (sunken panel)

15. Dentils (medallions)

———

READING COMPREHENSION
UNDERSTANDING AND INTERPRETING WRITTEN MATERIAL
EXAMINATION SECTION
TEST 1

DIRECTIONS: Each question or incomplete statement is followed by several suggested answers or completions. Select the one that BEST answers the question or completes the statement. *PRINT THE LETTER OF THE CORRECT ANSWER IN THE SPACE AT THE RIGHT.*

Questions 1-3.

DIRECTIONS: Questions 1 through 3, inclusive, are to be answered in accordance with the following paragraph.

All cement work contracts, more or less, in setting. The contraction in concrete walls and other structures causes fine cracks to develop at regular intervals. The tendency to contract increases in direct proportion to the quantity of cement in the concrete. A rich mixture will contract more than a lean mixture. A concrete wall which has been made of a very lean mixture and which has been built by filling only about one foot in depth of concrete in the form each day will frequently require close inspection to reveal the cracks.

1. According to the above paragraph,　　　　　　　　　　　　　　　　　　　　　　　　1.____

    A. shrinkage seldom occurs in concrete
    B. shrinkage occurs only in certain types of concrete
    C. by placing concrete at regular intervals, shrinkage may be avoided
    D. it is impossible to prevent shrinkage

2. According to the above paragraph, the one of the factors which reduces shrinkage in　　2.____
   concrete is the

    A. volume of concrete in wall
    B. height of each day's pour
    C. length of wall
    D. length and height of wall

3. According to the above paragraph, a rich mixture　　　　　　　　　　　　　　　　　3.____

    A. pours the easiest
    B. shows the largest amount of cracks
    C. is low in cement content
    D. need not be inspected since cracks are few

Questions 4-6.

DIRECTIONS: Questions 4 through 6, inclusive, are to be answered SOLELY on the basis of the following paragraph.

It is best to avoid surface water on freshly poured concrete in the first place. However, when there is a very small amount present, the recommended procedure is to allow it to evaporate before finishing. If there is considerable water, it is removed with a broom, belt, float, or by other convenient means. It is never good practice to sprinkle dry cement, or a mixture of cement and fine aggregate, on concrete to take up surface water. Such fine materials form a layer on the surface that is likely to dust or hair check when the concrete hardens.

4. The MAIN subject of the above passage is

   A. surface cracking of concrete
   B. evaporation of water from freshly poured concrete
   C. removing surface water from concrete
   D. final adjustments of ingredients in the concrete mix

5. According to the above passage, the sprinkling of dry cement on the surface of a concrete mix would MOST LIKELY

   A. prevent the mix from setting
   B. cause discoloration on the surface of the concrete
   C. cause the coarse aggregate to settle out too quickly
   D. cause powdering and small cracks on the surface of the concrete

6. According to the above passage, the thing to do when considerable surface water is present on the freshly poured concrete is to

   A. dump the concrete back into the mixer and drain the water
   B. allow the water to evaporate before finishing
   C. remove the water with a broom, belt, or float
   D. add more fine aggregate but not cement

Questions 7-9.

DIRECTIONS: Questions 7 through 9, inclusive, are to be answered ONLY in accordance with the information given in the paragraph below.

Before placing the concrete, check that the forms are rigid and well braced and place the concrete within 45 minutes after mixing it. Fill the forms to the top with the wearing-course concrete. Level off the surfaces with a strieboard. When the concrete becomes stiff but still workable (in a few hours), finish the surface with a wood float. This fills the hollows and compacts the concrete and produces a smooth but gritty finish. For a non-gritty and smoother surface (but one that is more slippery when wet), follow up with a steel trowel after the water sheen from the wood-troweling starts to disappear. If you wish, slant the tread forward a fraction of an inch so that it will shed rain water.

7. Slanting the tread a fraction of an inch gives a surface that will

   A. have added strength
   B. not be slippery when wet
   C. shed rain water
   D. not have hollows

8. In addition to giving a smooth but gritty finish, the use of a wood float will tend to 8.____

   A. give a finish that is slippery when wet
   B. compact the concrete
   C. give a better wearing course
   D. provide hollows to retain rain water

9. Which one of the following statements is most nearly correct? 9.____

   A. Having checked the forms, one may place the concrete immediately after mixing same.
   B. One must wait at least 15 minutes after mixing the concrete before it may be placed in the forms.
   C. A gritty compact finish and one which is more slippery when wet will result with the use of a wood float.
   D. A steel trowel used promptly after a wood float will tend to give a non-gritty smooth finish.

Questions 10-11.

DIRECTIONS: Questions 10 and 11 are to be answered SOLELY on the basis of information contained in the following paragraph.

Tools and plastering methods have changed very little over the years. Most of the changes are mere improvements of the basic tools. The tools formerly made by hand are now machine-made and are *rigidly* constructed of light, but strong, materials in contrast to the clumsy constructions of the early types. The power-driven mixers and hoisting equipment used on large plastering jobs today produce better mortars and lighten the tasks involved.

10. According to the above paragraph, present day tools used for plastering 10.____

    A. have made plastering much more complicated than it used to be
    B. are heavier than the old-fashioned tools they replaced
    C. produce poorer results but speed up the job
    D. are lighter and stronger than the hand-made tools of the past

11. As used in the above paragraph, the word *rigidly* means MOST NEARLY 11.____

    A. feeble   B. weakly   C. firmly   D. flexibly

Questions 12-18.

DIRECTIONS: Questions 12 through 18 are to be answered in accordance with the following paragraphs.

SURFACE RENEWING OVERLAYS

A surface renewing overlay should consist of material which can be constructed in very thin layers. The material must fill surface voids and provide an impervious skid-resistant surface. It must also be sufficiently resistant to traffic abrasion to provide an economical service life.

Materials meeting these requirements are:
  a. Asphalt concrete having small particle size
  b. Hot sand asphalts
  c. Surface seal coats

Fine-graded asphalt concrete or hot sand asphalt can be constructed in layers as thin as one-half inch and fulfill all requirements for surface renewing overlays. They are recommended for thin resurfacing of pavements having high traffic volumes, as their service lives are relatively long when constructed properly. They can be used for minor leveling, they are quiet riding, and their appearance is exceptionally pleasing. Seal coats or slurry seals may fulfill surface requirements for low traffic pavements.

12. A surface renewing overlay must fill surface voids, provide an impervious skid-resistant surface, and

   A. be resistant to traffic abrasion
   B. have small particle size
   C. be exceptionally pleasing in appearance
   D. be constructed in half-inch layers

13. An *impervious skid-resistant surface* means a surface that is

   A. rough to the touch and fixed firmly in place
   B. waterproof and provides good gripping for tires
   C. not damaged by skidding vehicles
   D. smooth to the touch and quiet riding

14. The number of types of materials that can be constructed in very thin layers and are also suitable for surface renewing overlays is

   A. 1   B. 2   C. 3   D. 4

15. The SMALLEST thickness of asphalt concrete or hot sand asphalt that can fulfill all requirements for surface renewing overlays is _____ inch(es).

   A. ¼   B. ½   C. 1   D. 2

16. The materials that are recommended for thin resurfacing of pavements having high traffic volumes are

   A. those that have relatively long service lives
   B. asphalt concretes with maximum particle size
   C. surface seal coats
   D. slurry seals with voids

17. Fine-graded asphalt concrete and hot sand asphalt are quiet riding and are also

   A. recommended for low traffic pavements
   B. used as slurry seal coats
   C. suitable for major leveling
   D. exceptionally pleasing in appearance

18. The materials that may fulfill surface requirements for low traffic pavements are 18._____
    A. fine-graded asphalt concretes
    B. hot sand asphalts
    C. seal coats or slurry seals
    D. those that can be used for minor leveling

Questions 19-25.

DIRECTIONS: Questions 19 through 25 are to be answered SOLELY on the basis of the paragraphs below.

OPEN-END WRENCHES

Solid, non-adjustable wrenches with openings in one or both ends are called open-end wrenches. Wrenches with small openings are usually shorter than wrenches with large openings. This proportions the lever advantage of the wrench to the bolt or stud and helps prevent wrench breakage or damage to the bolt or stud.

Open-end wrenches may have their jaws parallel to the handle or at angles anywhere up to 90 degrees. The average angle is 15 degrees. This angular displacement variation permits selection of a wrench suited for places where there is room to make only a part of a complete turn of a nut or bolt. Handles are usually straight, but may be curved. Those with curved handles are called S-wrenches. Other open-end wrenches may have offset handles. This allows the head to reach nut or bolt heads that are sunk below the surface.

There are a few basic rules that you should keep in mind when using wrenches. They are:
 I. ALWAYS use a wrench that fits the nut properly. Otherwise, the wrench may slip, or the nut may be damaged.
 II. Keep wrenches clean and free from oil. Otherwise, they may slip, resulting in possible serious injury to you or damage to the work.
 III. Do NOT increase the leverage of a wrench by placing a pipe over the handle. Increased leverage may damage the wrench or the work.

19. Open-end wrenches 19._____
    A. are adjustable
    B. are solid
    C. always have openings at both ends
    D. are always S-shaped

20. Wrench proportions are such that wrenches with _____ openings have _____ handles. 20._____
    A. larger; shorter   B. smaller; longer
    C. larger; longer   D. smaller; thicker

21. The average angle between the jaws and the handle of a wrench is _____ degrees. 21._____
    A. 0   B. 15   C. 22   D. 90

22. Offset handles are intended for use MAINLY with

    A. offset nuts
    B. bolts having fine threads
    C. nuts sunk below the surface
    D. bolts that permit limited swing

23. The wrench which is selected should fit the nut properly because this

    A. prevents distorting the wrench
    B. insures use of all wrench sizes
    C. avoids damaging the nut
    D. overstresses the bolt

24. Oil on wrenches is

    A. *good* because it prevents rust
    B. *good* because it permits easier turning
    C. *bad* because the wrench may slip off the nut
    D. *bad* because the oil may spoil the work

25. Extending the handle of a wrench by slipping a piece of pipe over it is considered

    A. *good* because it insures a tight nut
    B. *good* because less effort is needed to loosen a nut
    C. *bad* because the wrench may be damaged
    D. *bad* because the amount of tightening can not be controlled

---

KEY (CORRECT ANSWERS)

1.	D	11.	C
2.	B	12.	A
3.	B	13.	B
4.	C	14.	C
5.	D	15.	B
6.	C	16.	A
7.	C	17.	D
8.	B	18.	C
9.	A	19.	B
10.	D	20.	C

21. B
22. C
23. C
24. C
25. C

TEST 2

DIRECTIONS: Each question or incomplete statement is followed by several suggested answers or completions. Select the one that BEST answers the question or completes the statement. *PRINT THE LETTER OF THE CORRECT ANSWER IN THE SPACE AT THE RIGHT.*

Questions 1-3.

DIRECTIONS: Questions 1 through 3 are to be answered SOLELY on the basis of the following passage.

A utility plan is a floor plan which shows the layout of a heating, electrical, plumbing, or other utility system. Utility plans are used primarily by the persons reponsible for the utilities, but they are important to the craftsman as well. Most utility installations require the leaving of openings in walls, floors, and roofs for the admission or installation of utility features. The craftsman who is, for example, pouring a concrete foundation wall must study the utility plans to determine the number, sizes, and locations of the openings he must leave for piping, electric lines, and the like.

1. The one of the following items of information which is LEAST likely to be provided by a utility plan is the

    A. location of the joists and frame members around stairwells
    B. location of the hot water supply and return piping
    C. location of light fixtures
    D. number of openings in the floor for radiators

1._____

2. According to the passage, the persons who will *most likely* have the GREATEST need for the information included in a utility plan of a building are those who

    A. maintain and repair the heating system
    B. clean the premises
    C. paint housing exteriors
    D. advertise property for sale

2._____

3. According to the passage, a repair crew member should find it MOST helpful to consult a utility plan when information is needed about the

    A. thickness of all doors in the structure
    B. number of electrical outlets located throughout the structure
    C. dimensions of each window in the structure
    D. length of a roof rafter

3._____

Questions 4-9.

DIRECTIONS: Questions 4 through 9 are to be answered SOLELY on the basis of the following passage.

The basic hand-operated hoisting device is the tackle or purchase, consisting of a line called a fall, reeved through one or more blocks. To hoist a load of given size, you must set up a rig with a safe working load equal to or in excess of the load to be hoisted. In order to do this, you must be able to calculate the safe working load of a single part of line of given size, the safe working load of a given purchase which contains a line of given size, and the minimum size of hooks or shackles which you must use in a given type of purchase to hoist a given load. You must also be able to calculate the thrust which a given load will exert on a gin pole or a set of shears inclined at a given angle, the safe working load which a spar of a given size used as a gin pole or as one of a set of shears will sustain, and the stress which a given load will set up in the back guy of a gin pole or in the back guy of a set of shears inclined at a given angle.

4. The above passage refers to the lifting of loads by means of
   A. erected scaffolds
   B. manual rigging devices
   C. power-driven equipment
   D. conveyor belts

5. It can be concluded from the above passage that a set of shears serves to
   A. absorb the force and stress of the working load
   B. operate the tackle
   C. contain the working load
   D. compute the safe working load

6. According to the above passage, a spar can be used for a
   A. back guy   B. block   C. fall   D. gin pole

7. According to the above passage, the rule that a user of hand-operated tackle MUST follow is to make sure that the safe working load is AT LEAST
   A. equal to the weight of the given load
   B. twice the combined weight of the block and falls
   C. one-half the weight of the given load
   D. twice the weight of the given load

8. According to the above passage, the two parts that make up a tackle are
   A. back guys and gin poles
   B. blocks and falls
   C. rigs and shears
   D. spars and shackles

9. According to the above passage, in order to determine whether it is safe to hoist a particular load, you MUST
   A. use the maximum size hooks
   B. time the speed to bring a given load to a desired place
   C. calculate the forces exerted on various types of rigs
   D. repeatedly lift and lower various loads

Questions 10-15.

DIRECTIONS: Questions 10 through 15 are to be answered SOLELY on the basis of the following set of instructions.

PATCHING SIMPLE CRACKS IN A BUILT-UP ROOF

If there is a visible crack in built-up roofing, the repair is simple and straightforward:

1. With a brush, clean all loose gravel and dust out of the crack, and clean three or four inches around all sides of it.
2. With a trowel or putty knife, fill the crack with asphalt cement and then spread a layer of asphalt cement about 1/8 inch thick over the cleaned area.
3. Place a strip of roofing felt big enough to cover the crack into the wet cement and press it down firmly.
4. Spread a second layer of cement over the strip of felt and well past its edges.
5. Brush gravel back over the patch.

10. According to the above passage, in order to patch simple cracks in a built-up roof, it is necessary to use a

    A. putty knife and a drill
    B. knife and pliers
    C. tack hammer and a punch
    D. brush and a trowel

11. According to the above passage, the size of the area that should be clear of loose gravel and dust before the asphalt cement is first applied should

    A. be the exact size of the crack itself
    B. extend three or four inches on all sides of the crack
    C. be 1/8 inch greater than the size of the crack itself
    D. extend the length of the roofing strip

12. According to the above passage, loose gravel and dust in the crack should be removed with a

    A. brush   B. felt pad   C. trowel   D. dust mop

13. Assume that both layers of asphalt cement needed to patch the crack are of the same thickness.
    The total thickness of asphalt cement used in the patch should be MOST NEARLY _____ inch.

    A. 1/2   B. 1/3   C. 1/4   D. 1/8

14. According to the instructions in the above passage, how large should the strip of roofing felt be cut?

    A. Three of four inches square
    B. Smaller than the crack and small enough to be surrounded by cement on all sides of the strip
    C. Exactly the same size and shape of the area covered by the wet cement
    D. Large enough to completely cover the crack

15. The final or finishing action to be taken in patching a simple crack in a built-up roof is to

    A. clean out the inside of the crack
    B. spread a layer of asphalt a second time
    C. cover the crack with roofing felt
    D. cover the patch of roofing felt and cement with gravel

Questions 16-17.

DIRECTIONS: Questions 16 and 17 are to be answered SOLELY on the basis of the information given in the following paragraph.

Supplies are to be ordered from the stockroom once a week. The standard requisition form, Form SP21, is to be used for ordering all supplies. The form is prepared in triplicate, one white original and two green copies. The white and one green copy are sent to the stockroom, and the remaining green copy is to be kept by the orderer until the supplies are received.

16. According to the above paragraph, there is a limit on the

    A. amount of supplies that may be ordered
    B. day on which supplies may be ordered
    C. different kinds of supplies that may be ordered
    D. number of times supplies may be ordered in one year

17. According to the above paragraph, when the standard requisition form for supplies is prepared,

    A. a total of four requisition blanks is used
    B. a white form is the original
    C. each copy is printed in two colors
    D. one copy is kept by the stock clerk

Questions 18-21.

DIRECTION: Questions 18 through 21 are to be answered SOLELY on the basis of the following passage.

The Oil Pollution Act for U. S. waters defines an *oily mixture* as 100 parts or more of oil in one million parts of mixture. This mixture is not allowed to be discharged into the prohibited zone. The prohibited zone may, in special cases, be extended 100 miles out to sea but, in general, remains at 50 miles offshore. The United States Coast Guard must be contacted to report all *oily mixture* spills. The Federal Water Pollution Control Act provides for a fine of $10,000 for failure to notify the United States Coast Guard. An employer may take action against an employee if the employee causes an *oily mixture* spill. The law holds your employer responsible for either cleaning up or paying for the removal of the oil spillage.

18. According to the Oil Pollution Act, an *oily mixture* is defined as one in which there are _____ parts or more of oil in _____ parts of mixture.

    A. 50; 10,000
    B. 100; 10,000
    C. 100; 1,000,000
    D. 10,000; 1,000,000

19. Failure to notify the proper authorities of an *oily mixture* spill is punishable by a fine. Such fine is provided for by the

    A. United States Coast Guard
    B. Federal Water Pollution Control Act
    C. Oil Pollution Act
    D. United States Department of Environmental Protection

20. According to the law, the one responsible for the removal of an *oily mixture* spilled into U.S. waters is the

    A. employer
    B. employee
    C. U.S. Coast Guard
    D. U.S. Pollution Control Board

21. The *prohibited zone,* in general, is the body of water

    A. within 50 miles offshore
    B. beyond 100 miles offshore
    C. within 10,000 yards of the coastline
    D. beyond 10,000 yards from the coastline

Questions 22-25.

DIRECTIONS: Questions 22 through 25 are to be answered SOLELY on the basis of the following paragraph.

Synthetic detergents are materials produced from petroleum products or from animal or vegetable oils and fats. One of their advantages is the fact that they can be made to meet a particular cleaning problem by altering the foaming, wetting, and emulsifying properties of a cleaner. They are added to commonly used cleaning materials such as solvents, water, and alkalies to improve their cleaning performance. The adequate wetting of the surface to be cleaned is paramount in good cleaning performance. Because of the relatively high surface tension of water, it has poor wetting ability, unless its surface tension is decreased by addition of a detergent or soap. This allows water to flow into crevices and around small particles of soil, thus loosening them.

22. According to the above paragraph, synthetic detergents are made from all of the following EXCEPT

    A. petroleum products   B. vegetable oils
    C. surface tension oils   D. animal fats

23. According to the above paragraph, water's poor wetting ability is related to

    A. its low surface tension
    B. its high surface tension
    C. its vegetable oil content
    D. the amount of dirt on the surface to be cleaned

24. According to the above paragraph, synthetic detergents are added to all of the following EXCEPT

    A. alkalines   B. water   C. acids   D. solvents

25. According to the above paragraph, altering a property of a cleaner can give an advantage in meeting a certain cleaning problem.
The one of the following that is NOT a property altered by synthetic detergents is the cleaner's

    A. flow ability
    B. foaming property
    C. emulsifying property
    D. wetting ability

25._____

KEY (CORRECT ANSWERS)

1.	A	11.	B
2.	A	12.	A
3.	B	13.	C
4.	B	14.	D
5.	A	15.	D
6.	D	16.	D
7.	A	17.	B
8.	B	18.	C
9.	C	19.	B
10.	D	20.	A

21. A
22. C
23. B
24. C
25. A

ARITHMETICAL REASONING
EXAMINATION SECTION
TEST 1

DIRECTIONS: Each question or incomplete statement is followed by several suggested answers or completions. Select the one that BEST answers the question or completes the statement. *PRINT THE LETTER OF THE CORRECT ANSWER IN THE SPACE AT THE RIGHT.*

1. A room is 7'6" wide by 9'0" long with a ceiling height of 8'0". One gallon of flat paint will cover approximately 400 square feet of wall.
   The number of gallons of this paint required to paint the walls of this room, making no deductions for windows or doors, is MOST NEARLY _____ gallon.

   A. 1/4 B. 1/2 C. 2/3 D. 1

2. The cost of a certain job is broken down as follows:
   Materials $3,750
   Rental of equipment   1,200
   Labor   3,150
   The percentage of the total cost of the job that can be charged to materials is MOST NEARLY

   A. 40% B. 42% C. 44% D. 46%

3. By trial it is found that by using two cubic feet of sand, a 5 cubic foot batch of concrete is produced.
   Using the same proportions, the amount of sand required to produce 2 cubic yards of concrete is MOST NEARLY _____ cubic feet.

   A. 20 B. 22 C. 24 D. 26

4. It takes 4 men 6 days to do a certain job.
   Working at the same speed, the number of days it will take 3 men to do this job is

   A. 7 B. 8 C. 9 D. 10

5. The cost of rawl plugs is $27.50 per gross.
   The cost of 2,448 rawl plugs is

   A. $467.50 B. $472.50 C. $477.50 D. $482.50

6. A box contains an equal number of iron and brass castings. Each iron casting weighs 2 pounds, and each brass casting weighs 1 pound.
   If the box contents weigh 240 pounds, the number of brass pieces in the box is

   A. 40 B. 80 C. 120 D. 160

7. The sum of 5 feet 2 3/4 inches, 8 feet 1/2 inch, and 12 1/2 inches is _____ feet _____ inches.

   A. 25; 3 3/4   B. 14; 3 3/4
   C. 13; 5 3/4   D. 13; 3 3/4

69

8. A vertical cylindrical tank 4 feet in diameter and 5 feet high has a capacity of 470 gallons. The number of gallons in the tank when filled to a depth of 1'6" is NEAREST to

   A. 45 B. 95 C. 140 D. 180

   8._____

9. A crate contains 3 pieces of equipment weighing 43, 59, and 66 pounds, respectively. If the crate is lifted by 4 men each lifting one corner of the crate, the average number of pounds lifted by each of the men is

   A. 56 B. 51 C. 42 D. 36

   9._____

10. The sum of the following numbers, 1 3/4, 3 1/6, 5 1/2, 6 5/8, and 9 1/4, is closest to

    A. 26 1/8 B. 26 1/4 C. 26 1/2 D. 26 3/4

    10._____

11. If a piece of plywood measures 5'1 1/4" x 3'2 1/2", the number of square feet in this board is MOST NEARLY

    A. 15.8 B. 16.1 C. 16.4 D. 16.7

    11._____

12. Assume that in quantity purchases, the city receives a discount of 33 1/3%. If a one-gallon can of paint retails at $16.00 per gallon, the cost of 375 gallons of this paint is MOST NEARLY

    A. $3,997.50 B. $3,998.25 C. $3,999.00 D. $4,000,00

    12._____

13. Assume that eight barrels of cement together weigh a total of 3,004 pounds and 12 ounces.
    If there are four bags of cement per barrel, then the weight of one bag of cement is MOST NEARLY _____ pounds.

    A. 93.1 B. 93.5 C. 93.9 D. 94.3

    13._____

14. Assume that one man cuts 50 nameplates per hour, whereas his co-worker cuts 55 nameplates per hour.
    At the end of 7 hours, the first man will have cut fewer nameplates than the second man by

    A. 9.1% B. 9.5% C. 9.7% D. 9.9%

    14._____

15. The jaws of a vise close 3/16 of an inch for each turn of the screw.
    If the vise is open 6 inches, the number of turns required to close the jaw is

    A. 8 B. 16 C. 32 D. 64

    15._____

16. If the inside diameter of a pipe is 3/8 of an inch and the wall thickness is .091 inches, the outside diameter of the pipe is _____ inches.

    A. .193 B. .284 C. .466 D. .557

    16._____

17. If one dozen 1/8" welding rods cost $4.80, 37 rods would cost

    A. $14.40 B. $14.80 C. $15.20 D. $15.60

    17._____

18. The sum of the following numbers, 6 5/8, 3 3/4, 4 1/2, 5 1/8, is

    A. 19 3/4 B. 19 7/8 C. 20 D. 20 1/8

    18._____

19. The sum of 5 feet 4 1/4 inches, 8 feet 7 1/2 inches, and 13 feet 5 3/4 inches is _____ feet _____ inches. 19.____

    A. 26; 6 3/4   B. 27; 5 1/2%
    C. 27; 7 1/2   D. 28; 8 3/4

20. If the floor area of one shop is 17 feet by 19 feet 3 inches and the floor area of an adjacent shop is 22 feet by 28 feet 6 inches, then the total floor area of these two shops is MOST NEARLY _____ square feet. 20.____

    A. 856   B. 946   C. 948   D. 954

21. A carton contains 9 dozen drill bits. 21.____
    If a helper removes 73 drill bits, the number of bits remaining in the carton is

    A. 27   B. 35   C. 47   D. 62

22. One inch is MOST NEARLY equal to _____ feet. 22.____

    A. 0.8   B. 0.08   C. 0.008   D. 0.0008

23. The circumference of a circle is given by the formula C = 2πR, where C is the circumference, R is the radius, and π is approximately 3 1/7. 23.____
    The circumference of an oil drum having a diameter of one foot and nine inches is, therefore, about _____ inches.

    A. 132   B. 66   C. 33   D. 17

24. Tubing with an outside diameter of 2" and a wall thickness of 1/16" has an inside diameter which is 24.____

    A. 1 1/2"   B. 1 3/4"   C. 1 7/8"   D. 1 15/16"

25. The decimal which is NEAREST 33/64 is 25.____

    A. 0.516   B. 0.500   C. 0.643   D. 1.939

KEY (CORRECT ANSWERS)

1. C
2. D
3. B
4. B
5. A

6. B
7. B
8. C
9. C
10. B

11. C
12. D
13. C
14. A
15. C

16. D
17. B
18. C
19. B
20. D

21. B
22. B
23. B
24. C
25. A

SOLUTIONS TO PROBLEMS

1. The area of the four walls = (2) (7 1/2') (8') + (2)(9')(8') = 264 sq.ft. Then, 264÷400=.66 or about 2/3 gallon of paint.

2. $3750÷($3750+$1200+$3150)=$3750÷$8100 ≈ 46%

3. 2 cu.yds. = 54 cu.ft. Then, 54 ÷ 5 = 10.8. Finally, (10.8)(2) ≈ 22 cu.ft. of sand.

4. (4)(6) = 24 man-days. Then, 24 ÷ 3 = 8 days

5. 2440 ÷ 144 = 17 gross of plugs. Then, (17)($27.50) = $467.50

6. Each 3 lbs. in the box means 1 iron casting and 1 brass casting. Then, 240 lbs. ÷ 3 lbs. = 80. Thus, there are 80 iron castings and 80 brass castings.

7. 5 ft. 2 3/4 in. + 8 ft. 1/2 in. + 0 ft. 12 1/2 in. = 13 ft. 15 3/4 in. = 14 ft. 3 3/4 in.

8. 1 1/2 ft. ÷ 5 ft. = .3 Then, (470 gallons)(.3) ≈ 140 gallons

9. 43 + 59 + 66 = 168 lbs. Then, 168 ÷ 4 = 42 lbs.

10. $1\frac{3}{4}+3\frac{1}{6}+5\frac{1}{2}+6\frac{5}{8}+9\frac{1}{4} = 24\frac{55}{24} = 26\frac{7}{24}$, closest to 26 1/4

11. (5'1 1/4")(3'2 1/2") = (61.25")(38.5") = 2358.125 sq. in.
Since 1 sq.ft. = 144 sq. in., 2358.125 sq.in. ≈ 16.4 sq.ft.

12. (375)($16) = $6000. With a 33 1/3% discount, the cost becomes 67 2/3% of $6000 = $4000

13. (8)(4) = 32 bags of cement with a total weight of 3004.75 pounds. This means each bag weighs 3004.75 ÷ 32 ≈ 93.9 pounds.

14. In 7 hours, the first man cuts 350 nameplates, whereas the second man cuts 385 nameplates. The percentage pertaining to the amount done less by the first man is (35/385)(100) ≈ 9.1%

15. 6 in. ÷ $\frac{3}{16}$ in. = 32 turns required

16. Outside diameter = .375" + .091" + .091" = .557"

17. 37÷12=3.08$\overline{3}$ Then, (3.08$\overline{3}$)($4.80)=$14.80

18. $6\frac{5}{8}+3\frac{3}{4}+4\frac{1}{2}+5\frac{1}{8}=18\frac{16}{8}=20$

19. $5'4\frac{1}{4}" + 8'7\frac{1}{2}" + 13'5\frac{3}{4}" = 26'17\frac{1}{2}" = 27'5\frac{1}{2}"$

20. Total area = $(17)(19\frac{1}{4}) + (22)(28\frac{1}{2}) \approx 954$ sq.ft.

21. $(9)(12) - 73 = 35$ remaining drill bits

22. 1 inch = $\frac{1}{12}$ ft. = $.08\overline{3} \approx .08$ ft

23. $C = (2)(\pi)(10.5 \text{ in.}) = 21\pi$ inches ≈ 66 inches

24. Inside diameter = $2" - \frac{1}{16}" - \frac{1}{16}" = 1\frac{7}{8}"$

25. $\frac{33}{64} = .515625 \approx .516$

TEST 2

DIRECTIONS: Each question or incomplete statement is followed by several suggested answers or completions. Select the one that BEST answers the question or completes the statement. *PRINT THE LETTER OF THE CORRECT ANSWER IN THE SPACE AT THE RIGHT.*

1. A floor that is 9' wide by 12' long measures _____ square feet.   1.____
   A. 12　　　B. 21　　　C. 108　　　D. 150

2. The sum of 5 1/16, 4 1/4, 4 3/8, and 3 7/16 is   2.____
   A. 17 1/8　　　B. 17 7/16　　　C. 17 1/4　　　D. 17 3/8

3. From a length of pipe 6 feet 9 inches long, you are asked to cut a piece 4 feet 5 inches long.   3.____
   The length of the remainder, in inches, should be
   A. 24　　　B. 26　　　C. 28　　　D. 53

4. The jaws of a vise close 3/16 inch for each turn of the screw.   4.____
   If the vise is open 3 3/8 inches, then the number of turns needed to close the jaws is
   A. 16　　　B. 17　　　C. 18　　　D. 24

5. 627 cubic feet contains MOST NEARLY _____ cubic yards.   5.____
   A. 21　　　B. 22　　　C. 23　　　D. 24

6. The right angle shown at the right has been divided into three parts.   6.____
   The number of degrees in the unmarked part is
   A. 46
   B. 36
   C. 21
   D. 6

7. It ordinarily requires 5 days for 2 men to complete a certain job.   7.____
   If the management wants to have this work done in two days, the number of men required would be
   A. 10　　　B. 7　　　C. 6　　　D. 5

8. A room 20' x 25' in area with a ceiling height of 9'6" is to be painted. One gallon of paint will cover 400 square feet.   8.____
   The MINIMUM number of gallons necessary to give the four walls and the ceiling one coat of paint is
   A. 2　　　B. 3　　　C. 4　　　D. 5

9. An office has floor dimensions of 16 feet 6 inches wide by 22 feet 0 inches long.   9.____
   The floor area of this office, in square feet, is MOST NEARLY
   A. 143　　　B. 263　　　C. 363　　　D. 463

10. A supplier quotes a list price of $14.00 for a replacement part less discounts of 25, 10, and 5 percent.
    The cost of the item is MOST NEARLY

    A. $5.50   B. $6.00   C. $8.50   D. $9.00

11. An equipment rental allowance includes the rental charge plus 9%.
    If a piece of equipment is rented for 11 days at $36 per day, the total equipment allowance is MOST NEARLY

    A. $360   B. $390   C. $430   D. $450

12. A plumbing sketch is drawn to a scale of 1/8" = 1 foot.
    A horizontal water line measuring 6 3/4 inches on the sketch would be equivalent to _____ feet of water pipe.

    A. 27   B. 41   C. 54   D. 64

13. A rectangular yard is 50'0" long by 8'6" wide.
    The area of the yard, in square feet, is

    A. 420.0   B. 422.5   C. 425.0   D. 427.5

14. A rectangular court is 23'0" long by 9'6" wide.
    The length of the diagonal is MOST NEARLY

    A. 24'8"   B. 24'10"   C. 25'2"   D. 25'6"

15. Concrete weighs 150 pounds per cubic foot.
    A slab of concrete 6'0" long by 3'6" wide by 1'4" thick weighs MOST NEARLY _____ pounds.

    A. 4,150   B. 4,200   C. 4,250   D. 4,300

16. A building 32'0" by 65'0" occupies a lot 60'0" by 110'0".
    The ratio of building area to lot area is MOST NEARLY

    A. 0.32   B. 0.33   C. 0.34   D. 0.35

17. The decimal equivalent of 31/64 of an inch is MOST NEARLY

    A. 0.45   B. 0.46   C. 0.47   D. 0.48

18. The decimal equivalent of 27/32 is MOST NEARLY

    A. 0.813   B. 0.828   C. 0.844   D. 0.859

19. If a scaled measurement of 1'3" on the drawing of a sheet metal layout represents an actual length of 10'0", then the drawing has been made to a scale of _____ inch to the foot.

    A. 3/4   B. 1 1/4   C. 1 1/2   D. 1 3/4

20. If it takes 4 painters 5 1/2 days to do a certain paint job, then the time that it should take 5 painters working at the same speed to do the same job is MOST NEARLY _____ days.

    A. 3 1/2   B. 4   C. 4 1/2   D. 5

21. The number of square feet in a flat rectangular roof measuring 42'6" x 83'4" is MOST NEARLY

   A. 3,520   B. 3,530   C. 3,540   D. 3,550

22. The sum of the following dimensions, 3 5/8", 4 1/4", 6 5/16", 7 3/4", and 8 1/2", is

   A. 30 3/8"   B. 30 7/16"   C. 30 1/2"   D. 30 9/16"

23. Assume that 1 1/2 pounds of pitch are required for each square foot of roof.
    The number of pounds that would be required for a roof 55 feet by 96 feet is MOST NEARLY _____ pounds.

   A. 5,000   B. 6,000   C. 7,000   D. 8,000

24. A rectangular plot is 30 feet wide by 60 feet long.
    The length of the diagonal, in feet, is MOST NEARLY

   A. 68   B. 67   C. 66   D. 65

25. The volume, in cubic feet, of a room 8'6" wide by 10'6" long by 8'8" high is MOST NEARLY

   A. 770   B. 774   C. 778   D. 782

KEY (CORRECT ANSWERS)

1. C		11. C	
2. A		12. C	
3. C		13. C	
4. C		14. B	
5. C		15. B	
6. B		16. A	
7. D		17. D	
8. C		18. C	
9. C		19. C	
10. D		20. C	

21. C
22. B
23. D
24. B
25. B

SOLUTIONS TO PROBLEMS

1. (9')(12') = 108 sq.ft.

2. 5 1/16 + 4 1/4 + 4 3/8 + 3 7/16 = 16 18/16 = 17 1/8

3. 6 ft. 9 in. - 4 ft. 5 in. = 2 ft. 4 in. = 28 in.

4. $3\frac{3}{8} \div \frac{3}{16} = \frac{27}{8} \cdot \frac{16}{3} = 18$

5. Since 1 cu.yd. = 27 cu.ft., 627 cu. ft. ≈ 23 cu.yds.

6. The unmarked part = 90° - 33° - 21° = 36°

7. (5)(2) = 10 man-days. Then, 10 ÷ 2 = 5 men

8. The area of the four walls = (2)(20)(9 1/2) + (2)(25)(9 1/2) = 855 sq.ft.
   The area of the ceiling is (20)(25) = 500 sq.ft. Total area to be painted = 1355 sq.ft.
   Finally, 1355 ÷ 400 ≈ 3.3875 gallons, which means 4 gallons will need to be used.

9. (16 1/2')(22') = 363 sq.ft.

10. ($14.00)(.75)(.90)(.95) = $8.9775 ≈ $9.00

11. $36 + (.09)($36) = $39.24 Then, ($39.24)(11) ≈ $430

12. $6\frac{3}{4} \div \frac{1}{8} = (\frac{27}{4})(8) = 54$. Then, (54)(1 ft.) = 54 ft.

13. Area = (50')(8 1/2') = 425 sq. ft.

14. The diagonal = $\sqrt{(23)^2 + (9.5)^2} = \sqrt{619.25} \approx 24.885$ ft. ≈ 24 ft. 10 in.

15. (6')(3 1/2')(1 1/3') = 28 cu.ft. Then, (28)(150 pounds) = 4200 pounds

16. (32')(65') ÷ (60')(110') = 2080 ÷ 6600 = .3$\overline{15}$ ≈ .32

17. $\frac{31}{64} = .484375 \approx .48$

18. $\frac{27}{32} = .84375 \approx .844$

19. 1'3" ÷ 10 = 15" ÷ 10 = $1\frac{1}{2}$"

5 (#2)

20. $(4)(5\frac{1}{2}) = 22$ painter-days. Then, $22 \div 5 \approx 4.5$ days

21. $(42\frac{1}{2}')(83\frac{1}{3}') = 3541\frac{2}{3}$ sq.ft. ≈ 3540 sq.ft.

22. $3\frac{5}{8}" + 4\frac{1}{4}" + 6\frac{5}{16}" + 7\frac{3}{4}" + 8\frac{1}{2}" = 28\frac{39}{16}" = 30\frac{7}{16}"$

23. $(55)(96) = 5280$ sq.ft. Then, $(5280)(1\frac{1}{2}) = 7920 \approx 8000$ pounds

24. Diagonal = $\sqrt{30^2 + 60^2} = \sqrt{4500} \approx 67$ ft.

25. $(8\frac{1}{2}')(10\frac{1}{2}')(8\frac{2}{3}') = 773.5 \approx 774$ cu.ft.

TEST 3

DIRECTIONS: Each question or incomplete statement is followed by several suggested answers or completions. Select the one that BEST answers the question or completes the statement. *PRINT THE LETTER OF THE CORRECT ANSWER IN THE SPACE AT THE RIGHT.*

Questions 1-5.

DIRECTIONS: Questions 1 through 5, inclusive, are to be answered on the basis of the information given below. In answering these questions, refer to this information.

A crew of 5 painters are going to paint 55 rooms. They will be painting only the walls, which are all 10 feet high. The rooms have the following dimensions: 30 rooms are 25 ft. long and 15 ft. wide, and the remaining rooms are 20 ft. long and 15 ft. wide. All walls will be painted the same color and will require 2 coats. Coverage is 500 square feet per gallon. Each painter can cover 700 square feet of wall per day and works 7 hours per day.

1. Assume that 20% of the total wall surface consists of windows which are not to be painted.
   The total wall surface, in square feet, to be painted is MOST NEARLY

   A. 15,600   B. 21,800   C. 33,200   D. 41,500

   1._____

2. Assume the total wall surface to be painted is 49,500 square feet per coat of paint.
   The total number of gallons of paint needed for a complete job is MOST NEARLY

   A. 250   B. 200   C. 150   D. 100

   2._____

3. The total number of working days required for this crew to cover 49,500 square feet of wall surface with two coats of paint is MOST NEARLY

   A. 17   B. 23   C. 28   D. 35

   3._____

4. Assuming each painter earns $11.20 per hour, the total cost in painter's wages for a job which takes 21 working days to complete is MOST NEARLY

   A. $10,460   B. $8,240   C. $6,020   D. $4,720

   4._____

5. If two painters are sick for two days each and they are not replaced, the total time to complete this job would be extended APPROXIMATELY _____ day(s).

   A. 1   B. 2   C. 3   D. 4

   5._____

6. A rectangular wooden building occupies a ground space 27'6" long by 18'0" wide. The walls are 17'6" high. Ignoring window and door spaces, the outside area requiring painting is, in square feet, MOST NEARLY

   A. 1,570   B. 1,590   C. 1,610   D. 1,630

   6._____

2 (#3)

7. Assume that a certain type of cabinet can be painted in twenty minutes by using a brush and 15 min. by spraygun.
   Assuming that three painters are put on the job but only one spray gun is available, the number of hours required by the three painters to paint 100 cabinets, one using the spray gun and the other two using brushes, is MOST NEARLY

   A. 9 B. 10 C. 11 D. 12

   7.____

8. If it takes 5 painters 12 days to paint a building, the number of days it will take 9 painters to paint the same building, assuming all work is done at the same rate of speed, is MOST NEARLY

   A. 5 1/2 B. 6 1/2 C. 7 1/2 D. 8 1/2

   8.____

9. Assume that one gallon of paint, costing $12.50, is able to cover 500 square feet.
   If a painter can spread 1.25 gallons per day and receives $120 per day, the cost per 100 square feet for labor and paint for a one-coat application is MOST NEARLY

   A. $21.70 B. $24.20 C. $24.40 D. $24.60

   9.____

Questions 10-13.

DIRECTIONS: Questions 10 through 13 are to be answered on the basis of the information given below.

A crew of 6 painters is going to paint only the walls of 75 rooms. The rooms have the following dimensions: 50 rooms are 35 feet long, 20 feet wide, with walls 10 feet high; and 25 rooms are 25 feet long, 15 feet wide, with walls 10 feet high. The walls are to be given two coats. The paint coverage is 400 square feet per gallon per coat. Assume a painter can cover 650 square feet of wall per 7-hour day. Assume that wall surfaces have windows and doors which constitute 10% of the wall surfaces and are not to be painted.

10. The total wall surface to be painted per coat of paint is MOST NEARLY _____ square feet.

    A. 65,300 B. 67,500 C. 69,500 D. 71,100

    10.____

11. Assume that the total wall surface to be painted is 75,000 square feet.
    The total number of gallons of paint needed for a complete job, neglecting any waste, is MOST NEARLY

    A. 358 B. 364 C. 370 D. 375

    11.____

12. The total number of working days required for the crew to cover 75,000 square feet of wall surface with 2 coats of paint is MOST NEARLY _____ days.

    A. 37 B. 38 C. 41 D. 43

    12.____

13. If a painter earns $7.35 per hour for a 7-hour day, then the TOTAL cost in painter's wages for a job that takes 27 working days for the 6-man crew is

    A. $8,156.40   B. $8,255.40
    C. $8,334.90   D. $8,456.70

    13.____

14. Assume that you assign 3 painters to do a job in 12 days. After 4 days, you add 3 more painters, all of whom work at the same pace.
    How many additional days will it take the 6 men to do the job?

    A. 2   B. 3   C. 4   D. 5

15. Assume that a given paint has a covering capacity of 375 square feet per gallon. In order to paint 10,125 square feet, you would need _____ gallons.

    A. 21   B. 23   C. 25   D. 27

16. The sum of the following dimensions, 3'2 1/4", 0'8 7/8", 2'6 3/8", 2'9 3/4", and 1'0", is

    A. 9'2 7/8"   B. 10'3 1/4" C. 10'7 3/8" D. 11'4 1/4"

17. If the scale of a drawing is 1/8" to the foot, then a 1/2" measurement on the drawing would represent an actual length of _____ feet.

    A. 2   B. 4   C. 8   D. 16

18. The average 40-hour weekly pay of 3 painters who earn $8.50, $9.00, and $9.50 an hour is

    A. $340   B. $360   C. $380   D. $400

19. If it takes 10 gallons of paint to cover a 1,500 square foot room, how many gallons of paint will be needed to paint a 3,750 square foot room?

    A. 20   B. 22   C. 25   D. 27

20. A maintenance man is getting a 5% raise on his $8.00 an hour wage. What will be his weekly earnings if he works a 44-hour week and is paid 1 1/2 times for hours over 40 hours?

    A. $320   B. $336   C. $369.60   D. $386.40

KEY (CORRECT ANSWERS)

1. C		11. D	
2. B		12. B	
3. C		13. C	
4. B		14. C	
5. A		15. D	
6. B		16. B	
7. B		17. B	
8. B		18. B	
9. A		19. C	
10. B		20. D	

SOLUTIONS TO PROBLEMS

1. Total area of the walls in all 55 rooms = [(2)(25)(10)+(2)(10)(15)] [30] + [(2)(10)(20)+(2)(10)(15)][25] = 24,000 + 17,500 = 41,500 sq.ft. Since 20% of the wall surface consists of windows, the wall surface to be painted = (.80)(41,500) = 33,200 sq.ft.

2. $49,500 \div 500 = 99$ gallons required for 1 coat of paint. Then, $(2)(99) \approx 200$ gallons will be needed for 2 coats of paint.

3. (700)(5) = 3500 sq.ft. can be covered each day with 1 coat of paint. To cover 49,500 sq.ft. with 2 coats of paint will require $(49,500 \div 3500)(2) \approx 28$ days.

4. Total cost = (5)($11.20)(7)(21) = $8232, which is nearest to answer B ($8240).

5. (5)(21) = 105 man-days. If 2 painters are sick for 2 days, a total of (3)(21) + (2)(19) = 101 man-days. The remaining 4 man-days will be done by 3 painters, and this will take $4 \div 3 = 1\frac{1}{3} \approx 1$ more day.

6. (2)(27 1/2')(17 1/2') + (2)(18')(17 1/2') = 1592 ≈ 1590 sq.ft.

7. The spray painter paints 4 cabinets/hr. [60÷15=4]; the brush painters each paint 3 cabinets/hr. [60÷20=3]; ten cabinets/hr. for 10 hrs. = 100 cabinets.

8. (5)(12) = 60 man-days. Then, $60 \div 9 = 6\frac{2}{3} \approx 6\frac{1}{2}$ 64 days

9. In one day, a painter can cover (500)(1.25) = 625 sq.ft.
Labor cost per 100 sq.ft. = $120 ÷ 6.25 = $19.20
Paint cost per 100 sq.ft. = 12.50 ÷ 5 = $2.50
Total cost (per 100 sq.ft.) of labor and paint = $21.70

10. Total area of the walls in 75 rooms = [50][(2)(10)(35)+(2)(10)(20)] + [25][(2)(10)(25)+(2)(15)(10)] = 55,000 + 20,000 = 75,000 sq.ft. Since 10% of this area will not be painted, the amount of area to be painted = (.90)(75,000) = 67,500 sq.ft.

11. 75,000 ÷ 400 = 187.5 gallons required for 1 coat of paint. Then, (187.5)(2) = 375 gallons will be needed for 2 coats of paint.

12. (6)(650) = 3900 sq.ft. can be covered each day with 1 coat of paint. To cover 75,000 sq.ft. with 2 coats of paint will require $(75,000 \div 3900)(2) \approx 38$ days.

13. Total cost = (6)($7.35)(7)(27) = $8334.90

14. (3)(12) = 36 man-days. After 4 days, (3)(4) = 12 man-days have been used, which means 24 man-days are left to complete the job. If 6 men are used for the remainder of this job, 24 ÷ 6 = 4 more days will be needed.

15. 10,125 ÷ 375 = 27 gallons

16. 3'2 1/4" + 0'8 7/8" + 2'6 3/8" + 2'9 3/4" + 1'0" = 8'25 18/8" = 10'3 1/4"

17. $\frac{1}{2}" \div \frac{1}{8}" = 4$. So, the actual length is 4 ft.

18. [(40)($8.50)+(40)($9.00)+(40)($9.50)] ÷ 3 = $360

19. 3750 ÷ 1500 = 2.5 Then, (2.5)(10) = 25 gallons

20. ($8.00)(1.05) = $8.40/hr. for regular pay and ($8.40)(1.5) = $12.60/hr. overtime. Total pay = ($8.40)(40) + ($12.60)(4) = $386.40

BASIC FUNDAMENTALS OF PLASTERING, STUCCOING AND TILE SETTING

TABLE OF CONTENTS

		Page
I.	Plaster Ingredients	1
II.	Plaster Bases	4
III.	Mixing Plaster	6
IV.	Applying Plaster	9
V.	Ceramic Wall Tile	14
VI.	General Hints on Stuccoing	15

BASIC FUNDAMENTALS OF
PLASTERING, STUCCOING AND TILE SETTING

PLASTER and STUCCO, like concrete, are construction materials which are applied in a plastic condition, and which harden in place after being applied. The fundamental difference between plaster and stucco is simply one of location; if the material is used internally it is called plaster; if it is used externally it is called stucco.

Again like concrete, the active ingredient in plaster is a CEMENTITIOUS material, or BINDER. If plaster is applied in more than one layer, the top layer is called the FINISH COAT and each of the lower layers is a BASE COAT. Plaster for a finish coat may consist of binder alone; however, most finish coat plaster and most base coat plaster contains AGGREGATE as well as binder. Plaster aggregate may consist of sand or one of several other materials. The aggregate in plaster, like the aggregate in concrete, provides additional bulk and stability.

You can see that plaster is to a large extent very much like concrete. The principal difference lies in the fact that concrete can, because of its high compressive strength, be used as a load-bearing structural material. The considerably lower strength of plaster has, up until now, confined its use principally to finish. However, experiments are being conducted with an eye to developing plasters with load-bearing strength.

A plaster mix, like a concrete mix, is made plastic for application by the addition of water to the dry ingredients. Again like concrete, it is a reaction of the binder to the water called HYDRATION that causes the mix to harden.

I. PLASTER INGREDIENTS

The binders most commonly used for plaster are GYPSUM, LIME, and PORTLAND CEMENT. Because gypsum plaster should not be exposed to free water or severe moisture conditions, it is usually confined to interior use. Lime and portland cement plaster may be used both internally and externally.

GYPSUM PLASTER

Gypsum is a naturally occurring sedimentary gray, white, or pink rock. The natural rock is crushed and then heated to high temperature, a process (known as CALCINING) which drives off about three-quarters of the WATER OF CRYSTALLIZATION which forms about 20 percent by weight of the rock in a natural state. The calcined material is then ground to a fine powder, to which certain ADDITIVES are added to control set, stabilization, and other physical or chemical characteristics.

For a type of gypsum plaster called KEENE'S CEMENT the crushed gypsum rock is heated until nearly all of the water of crystallization is driven off. To offset slow-setting caused by absence of so much WATER OF HYDRATION, an Englishman named Keene patented a process of adding alum as an accelerator. The resulting plaster, called Keene's cement, produces a very hard, fine-textured finish coat.

The removal of water of crystallization from natural gypsum is a DEHYDRATION process. In the course of setting, mixing water (water of hydration) added to the mix REHYDRATES with the gypsum, thus causing RECRYSTALLIZATION. Recrystallization causes the plaster to harden.

There are four common types of gypsum basecoat plasters, as follows:

GYPSUM NEAT plaster is gypsum plaster without aggregate, intended for mixing with aggregate on the job.

GYPSUM READY-MIXED plaster consists of gypsum and ordinary mineral aggregate; at the job it requires addition of only the water.

GYPSUM WOOD-FIBERED plaster consists of calcined gypsum combined with not less than 0.75 percent by weight of non-staining wood fibers. It may be used as is or mixed with 1 part sand to produce base coats of superior strength and hardness.

GYPSUM BOND plaster is so-called because it is designed to bond to properly prepared monolithic concrete. It consists essentially of calcined gypsum mixed with from 2 to 5 percent of lime by weight.

There are five common types of gypsum finish coat plasters, as follows:

READY-MIX GYPSUM FINISH plasters are designed for use over gypsum plaster basecoats. They consist of finely ground calcined gypsum, some with and others without aggregate. At the job they require addition of water only.

GYPSUM ACOUSTICAL plasters are designed to reduce sound reverberation.

GYPSUM GAUGING plasters contain LIME PUTTY, the inclusion of which provides certain setting properties, increases dimensional stability during drying, and provides initial surface hardness. Gauging plasters are obtainable as SLOW-SET, QUICK-SET, and SPECIAL HIGH STRENGTH.

GYPSUM MOLDING plaster is used primarily in casting and ornamental plaster work. It is available neat (that is, without admixtures) or with lime. As with portland cement mortar, the addition of lime to a plaster mix makes the mix more "buttery."

KEENE'S CEMENT is a fine, high density plaster capable of creating a highly polished surface. It is customarily used with lime putty, and with fine sand which provides crack-resistance.

LIME PLASTER

LIME is obtained principally from the burning (called calcining) of LIMESTONE, a very common mineral. During the calcining process certain chemical changes occur which transform the limestone into what is called QUICK-LIME. Quicklime which meets certain requirements is pulverized for building use; other quicklime is further processed into HYDRATED lime for building use.

Before being used for plastering, quicklime must be SLAKED. Slaking consists of adding the quicklime to water. Be careful when adding quicklime to water because of a chemical change that will occur. For example, always add quick-slaking lime to water; when escaping steam appears, the lime should be hoed and just enough lime added to stop the steaming. When mixing medium-slaking and slow-slaking limes, the water should be added to the lime. The slow-slaking lime must be mixed under an ideal temperature; thereby making it necessary to heat the water in cold weather. Magnesium lime is easily "drowned" so be careful when adding too much water to quick-slaking calcium lime. When too little water is added to either calcium or magnesium limes they can be "burned." Whenever lime is burned or drowned, a part of it is spoiled and it will not harden and the paste is not as viscous and plastic as it should be. The quicklime must be soaked for an extended period of as much as 21 days. The end-product is plastic LIME PUTTY.

Because of the delays involved in the slaking process, most building lime is hydrated lime. NORMAL hydrated lime is converted into lime putty by soaking for at least 16 hours. SPECIAL hydrated lime develops immediate plasticity when mixed with water and may be used right after mixing.

Like calcined gypsum, lime plaster tends to return to its original rock-like state after application.

For interior basecoat work, lime plaster has been largely supplanted by gypsum plaster. It is now used principally for interior finish coats. Because lime putty is the most plastic and workable of the cementitious materials used in plaster, it is often added to other less workable plaster materials to improve plasticity. For lime plaster, lime (in the form of either dry hydrate or lime putty) is mixed with sand, water, and a GAUGING MATERIAL. A gauging material is intended to produce early strength and to counteract shrinkage tendencies. The gauging material may be either GYPSUM GAUGING PLASTER or Keene's cement for interior work, or portland cement for exterior work.

PORTLAND CEMENT

Portland cement plaster is similar to the portland cement mortar used in masonry. It may contain cement, sand, and water only; however, lime, ground asbestos, or some other plasticizing material is usually added for "butteriness."

Portland cement plaster may be applied direct to exterior and interior masonry walls. Elsewhere it will be applied over metal lath. Never apply portland cement plaster over gypsum plasterboard or over gypsum tile. Portland cement plaster is recommended for use in plastering walls and ceilings of large walk-in refrigerators and cold storage spaces, basement spaces, toilets, showers, and similar areas where an extra hard or highly water-resistant surface is required.

AGGREGATE

The aggregates most commonly used in plaster are SAND, VERMICULITE, and PERLITE. Generally speaking, any sand retained on the No. 4 sieve is too coarse to use in plaster, and only a small percentage of the material (about 5 percent) should pass the No. 200 sieve.

Sand

Sand for plaster, like sand for concrete, must be free of more than a specified minimum of organic impurities and harmful chemicals. Certain tests for these impurities and chemicals are conducted by qualified personnel.

Proper aggregate gradation influences plaster strength and workability, and likewise has an effect on the tendency of the material to shrink or expand while setting. For sand intended for use in gypsum plaster, recommended gradation is as follows:

Sieve Size	Percentage Retained by Weight	
	Max	Min
No. 4	0	-
No. 8	5	0
No. 16	30	5
No. 30	65	30
No. 50	95	65
No. 100	100	90

For sand intended for use in exterior plaster, recommended gradation is as follows:

Sieve Size	Percentage Retained by Weight	
	Max	Min
No. 4	0	-
No. 8	10	0
No. 16	40	10
No. 30	65	30
No. 50	90	70
No. 100	100	95

Plaster strength is reduced if excessive fine aggregate material is present in a mix. The greater quantity of mixing water required raises the water:cement ratio, thereby reducing the dry set density. The cementitious material becomes overextended, because it must coat a relatively larger overall aggregate surface.

An excess of coarse adversely affects workability; the mix becomes "harsh working" and difficult to apply.

Plaster shrinkage during drying may be caused by an excess of either fine or coarse. Because an excess of fine increases the aggregate total surface area, a larger quantity of binder paste is needed to coat all particles. The mix becomes too rich in cementitious material, and it is the cementitious material which is unstable after application. The end-effect is much the same if there is too much coarse; in this case, there is not enough fine to fill the voids between coarse particles, and more cementitious material must be used to fill these voids. Again the result is a rich and relatively unstable material.

Vermiculite

VERMICULITE is a MICACEOUS mineral—meaning a mineral in which each particle is LAMINATED, or made up of adjoining layers. When vermiculite particles are exposed to intense heat, steam forms between the layers so as to force them apart; this causes each particle to increase from 6 to 20 times in volume. The expanded material is soft and pliable, with a color varying between silver and gold.

For ordinary plaster work, vermiculite is used only with gypsum plaster—therefore, in general, only for interior plastering. For acoustical plaster, vermiculite is combined with a special acoustical binder.

Expanded vermiculite is manufactured in five types (I, II, III, IV, and V) according to particle size. Only type III is used in plastering. It is the lightest of the standard plaster aggregates, weighing only from 6 to 10 lbs per cu ft. The approximate dry weight of a cu ft of 1:2 gypsum-vermiculite plaster is 50 to 55 lbs; the dry weight of a cu ft of comparable sanded plaster is 104 to 120 lbs.

For gypsum-vermiculite plaster the following gradation for the vermiculite is recommended:

PLASTERING, STUCCOING AND TILE SETTING

	Percentage Retained by Volume	
Sieve Size	Max	Min
No. 4	0	-
No. 8	10	0
No. 16	75	40
No. 30	95	65
No. 50	98	75
No. 100	100	90

Perlite

Raw perlite is a volcanic glass which, when flash-roasted, expands to form frothy particles of irregular shape that contain countless minute air cells. Perlite ore is crushed and then heated to high temperature; as the particles soften, combined water turns to steam. This causes the particles to "pop," forming a frothy mass of glass bubbles 4 to 20 times the volume of the raw particle. The process is called EXPANDING; the color of expanded perlite ranges from pearly white to grayish white.

Perlite is used with calcined gypsum or portland cement for interior plastering; it is also used with special binders for acoustical plaster. The approximate dry weight of a cu ft of 1:2 gypsum-perlite plaster is 50 to 55 lbs, or about half the weight of a cu ft of sand-plaster.

For gypsum-perlite plaster the recommended gradation for the perlite is as follows:

	Percentage Retained by Volume	
Sieve Size	Max	Min
No. 4	0	-
No. 8	5	0
No. 16	60	10
No. 30	95	45
No. 50	98	75
No. 100	100	88

Other Aggregates

Although sand, vermiculite, and perlite constitute the great preponderance of plaster aggregate, certain other materials are used. Wood fiber may be added to neat gypsum plaster at the time of manufacture, to improve the working qualities of the gypsum. PUMICE is a naturally foamed volcanic glass similar to perlite, but heavier (28 to 32 lbs per cu ft, against 7.5 to 15 lbs for perlite). The weight differential gives perlite an economic advantage, and limits the use of pumice to localities near where it is produced.

WATER

The mixing water in plaster performs two functions. First, it transforms the dry ingredients into a plastic, workable mass; second, it combines mechanically and/or chemically with the binder to induce hardening. As is the case with concrete, there is a maximum quantity of water per unit of binder required for complete hydration, and an excess over this amount reduces the plaster strength below the maximum attainable.

However, in all plaster mixing more water is added than is necessary for complete hydration of the binder; the excess is necessary to bring the mix to workable consistency. The amount that must be added for workability depends on the character and age of the binder, the method of application, the drying conditions, and the tendency of the base to absorb water. A porous masonry base, for example, will draw a good deal of water out of a plaster mix. If this reduces the water content of the mix, below the maximum required for hydration, incomplete curing will result.

As a general rule, only the amount of water required to attain workability is added to a mix, and no more. The water should be clean and fresh, and it must contain no dissolved chemicals which might accelerate or retard the set. Water previously used to wash plastering tools should never be used for mixing plaster; such water may contain particles of set plaster which may accelerate setting. Stagnant water should be avoided, because such water may contain organic material which may retard setting and possibly cause staining.

II. PLASTER BASES

For plastering there must be a continuous surface to which the plaster can be applied and to which it will cling; such a surface is called a plaster BASE. A continuous concrete or masonry surface may serve as a base without the necessity for further treatment.

For plaster planes such as those defined by the inner edges of studs or the lower edges of joists, however, base material must be installed to form a continuous surface which will span the spaces between the structural members. Material of this kind is called LATH. Lath formerly consisted of thin wooden strips which were nailed at right angles to the studs or joists. Narrow openings were left between adjacent laths, through which the plaster penetrated to form a KEY which bonded the plaster to the lath.

In modern plastering, wooden lath has been almost entirely superseded by GYPSUM lath and METAL lath.

GYPSUM LATH

Gypsum lath is made by sandwiching a core of gypsum plaster between two sheets of a fibrous, absorbent paper. For PLAIN (non-perforated) gypsum lath, bond is effected by absorption or suction of the face of the lath. This absorption draws in some of the cementitious material in the plaster. As the plaster sets, particles of this absorbed material interlock with nonabsorbed particles in the plaster. For PERFORATED (punched with 3/4-in. holes 4 in. apart) gypsum plaster, suction bond is supplemented by keys formed by plaster which penetrates the holes.

Standard sheet size for gypsum lath is 16 in. x 48 in., except in the western U.S., where it is 16 1/5 in. x 48 in. LONG LENGTH gypsum lath comes 16 or 24 in. wide and any length up to 12 ft as ordered. Available thicknesses are 3/8 in. and 1/2 in. INSULATING gypsum lath has aluminum foil bonded to the back of the sheet; this material provides thermal insulation and also serves as a vapor barrier.

Gypsum lath is nailed to studs, joists, or furring strips with 1 1/8-in. to 1-1/4 in. flat-headed GYPSUM LATH NAILS, 5 nails to each stud, joist, or strip crossing. It may also be attached with power-driven staples.

METAL LATH

Metal lath consists essentially of a metal screen. Bond is created by keys formed by plaster forced through the screen openings; as the plaster hardens, it and the metal become rigidly interlocked.

WIRE lath consists simply of wire screen, formed by weaving or welding intersecting wires together. SHEET metal lath consists of sheet metal perforated with openings of various shapes. EXPANDED metal lath is manufactured by first cutting staggered slits in a sheet and then expanding (stretching) the sheet to form the screen openings. RIB EXPANDED metal lath contains V-shaped metal ribs for the purpose of furring the lath out from the surface to which it is attached. Ordinary unribbed expanded metal lath is called FLAT EXPANDED.

Types of Flat Expanded Lath

DIAMOND MESH lath, suitable for all types of plastering, comes in 24-in. x 96-in. and 27-in. x 96- in. sheets.

SELF-FURRING DIAMOND MESH contains DIMPLES which fur it out 1/4 in. from the surface to which it is attached. This lath may be nailed to smooth concrete or masonry surfaces, or wrapped around structural steel, without the necessity for previous furring. It is widely used for replastering old walls and ceilings when the removal of the old plaster is not desired. Standard sizes are the same as for diamond mesh.

PAPER-BACKED DIAMOND MESH is designed to receive plaster applied by machine.

STUCCO MESH has larger openings than diamond mesh; it is intended primarily for exterior plastering.

Types of Rib Expanded Lath

FLAT rib lath has ribs 1/8 in. deep; THREE-EIGHTHS INCH rib lath has ribs 3/8 in. deep; and THREE-QUARTER INCH rib lath has ribs 3/4 in. deep. Standard sheet sizes for flat and three-eighths are the same as for diamond mesh. For three-quarter the widths are the same, but lengths of 120 in. and 144 in. are available besides 96 in.

Attachment of Metal Lath

Metal lath is nailed to vertical wooden supports (such as wall studs cr wall furring strips) with 4d common nails. It is nailed to horizontal wooden supports (such as ceiling joists or ceiling furring strips) with 1 1/2-in. barbed roofing nails. It may also be attached to wooden supports with power-driven staples. For attachment to metal supports, tie wires are used.

LATHING ACCESSORIES

LATHING ACCESSORIES consist of STRUCTURAL COMPONENTS and MISCELLANEOUS

ACCESSORIES. The principal use of structural components is in the construction of HOLLOW PARTITIONS. A hollow partition is one which contains no building framing members (such as studs and plates). Structural components are lathing accessories which take the place of the missing framing members in supporting the lath. They include prefabricated METAL STUDS and floor and ceiling RUNNER TRACKS. The runner tracks take the place of missing stud top and bottom plates; they usually consist of metal CHANNELS. Channels are also used for furring and bracing.

Miscellaneous accessories consist principally of various devices which are attached to the lath at corner and other locations, and which serve to define and reinforce corners, to provide dividing strips between plaster and the edges of baseboard or other trim, or to define plaster edges at unframed openings. CORNER BEADS are the most common miscellaneous accessories. Figure 1 shows a STANDARD FLANGE corner bead, in which the flanges are perforated metal. There are also EXPANDED FLANGE and WIDE FLANGE corner beads. CASING BEADS are similar devices for providing dividing strips between plaster edges and the edges of door and window casing. BASE BEADS (also called BASE SCREEDS) provide dividing strips between plaster edges and the edges of baseboards. All of these devices are attached to the lath before plaster is applied.

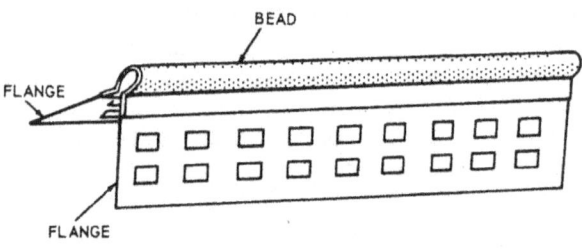

Figure 1.—Standard flange corner bead.

GROUNDS AND SCREEDS

GROUNDS are narrow strips of wood or metal that are placed around, and parallel to, the edges of surfaces and openings within the area to be plastered, principally to ensure that plaster will be applied to the correct thickness in locations where variations in thickness would be especially noticeable. The grounds are designed to be used as guides for the plastering straightedge when the final basecoat is brought to the required thickness and line. Such miscellaneous accessories as casing beads and base beads serve as grounds, in addition to providing dividing strips between plaster edges and the edges of trim.

Edges of door and window jambs are often used as grounds; however, it is not advisable to plaster directly to the wood in such cases. Contact between the dimensionally unstable wood and the more stable plaster produces differential movement (additionally complicated by the shock of opening and closing of door or window) which may damage plaster edges. If casing beads are not used, the plaster should be struck away from the wooden jamb after the surface has been leveled.

PLASTER SCREEDS are grounds consisting of narrow strips of plaster 4 to 6 in. wide, placed at intervals on large wall or ceiling areas. DOTS of plaster of the proper thickness are placed first, then connected by bands of the proper thickness. The spaces between the bands are then filled in, after the band (that is, the screeds) have hardened enough to support the plastering straightedge. Dampness will damage plaster; therefore, plaster should not be applied directly to exterior masonry walls. However, in such a case, it is advisable to fur the plaster at least 1 inch from the masonry.

III. MIXING PLASTER

Much plaster comes ready-mixed, requiring only the addition of enough water on the job to attain minimum required workability. For job-mixing, tables are available which give recommended ingredient proportions for gypsum, lime, lime-portland cement, and portland cement plaster for base coats on lath or on various types of concrete or masonry surfaces, and for finish coats of various types. This course can present recommended proportions for only the more common types of plastering situations. In the following sections, 1 part of cementitious material means 100 lbs (1 sack) gypsum, 100 lbs (2 sacks) hydrated lime, 1 cu ft lime putty, or 94 lbs (1 sack) portland cement. One part of aggregate means 100 lbs sand or 1 cu ft vermiculite or perlite. Vermiculite and perlite are not used with lime plaster; therefore, while aggregate parts given for gypsum or portland cement plaster may be presumed to refer to either sand or vermiculite/perlite, aggregate parts given for lime plaster mean sand only.

BASE COAT PROPORTIONS

TWO-COAT plaster work consists of a single base coat and a finish coat. THREE-COAT work consists of two base coats (the first called the SCRATCH coat, the second the BROWN coat) and a finish coat.

Portland cement plaster cannot be applied to a gypsum base. Lime plaster can in theory, but in practice only gypsum plaster is applied to gypsum lath as a base coat. For two-coat work on gypsum lath, the recommended base coat proportions for gypsum plaster are 1:2.5.

For two-coat work on a masonry (using this term to mean either monolithic concrete or masonry) base the recommended base coat proportions are as follows:

Gypsum plaster: 1:3
Lime plaster using hydrated lime: 1:7.5
Lime plaster using lime putty: 1:3.5

Portland cement plaster is not used for two-coat work, and two-coat work is not usually done on metal lath.

For three-coat work on gypsum lath the recommended base coat proportions for gypsum plaster are: scratch coat 1:2, brown coat 1:3; or both coats 1:2.5.

For three-coat work on metal lath the recommended base coat proportions are as follows:

Gypsum plaster: same as for three-coat work on gypsum lath
Lime plaster using hydrated lime: scratch 1:6.75, brown 1:9
Lime plaster using lime putty: scratch 1:3, brown 1:4
Portland cement plaster: both coats 1:3 to 1:5

For three-coat work on a masonry base the recommended base coat proportions are as follows:

Gypsum plaster: both coats 1:3
Portland cement plaster: both coats 1:3 to 1:5

Lime plaster is not usually used for three-coat work on a masonry base.

FINISH COAT PROPORTIONS

A lime finish may be applied over a lime, gypsum, or portland cement base coat; other finishes, however, should be applied only to basecoats containing the same cementitious material. A gypsum-vermiculite finish should be applied only to a gypsum-vermiculite basecoat.

Finish coat proportions vary according to whether the surface is to be finished with a TROWEL or with a FLOAT. These tools are described later. The trowel attains a smooth finish; the float attains a finish of a desired texture.

For a trowel-finish coat using gypsum plaster the recommended proportions are 200 lbs hydrated lime or 5 cu ft lime putty to 100 lbs gypsum gauging plaster.

For a trowel-finish coat using lime-Keene's cement plaster the recommended proportions are, for a medium-hard finish, 50 lbs hydrated lime or 100 lbs lime putty to 100 lbs Keene's cement. For a hard finish the recommended proportions are 25 lbs hydrated lime or 50 lbs lime putty to 100 lbs Keene's cement.

For a trowel-finish coat using lime-portland cement plaster the recommended proportions are 200 lbs hydrated lime or 5 cu ft lime putty to 94 lbs portland cement.

For a finish coat using portland cement-sand plaster the recommended ingredient proportions are 300 lbs sand to 94 lbs portland cement. This plaster may be either trowled or floated. Hydrated lime up to 10 percent by weight of the portland cement, or lime putty up to 25 percent of the volume of the portland cement, may be added as a plasticizer.

For a trowel-finish coat using gypsum gauging or gypsum neat plaster and vermiculite aggregate the recommended proportions are 1 cu ft vermiculite to 100 lbs plaster.

Recommended proportions for various types of float-finish coats are as follows:

Lime putty 2: Keene's cement 1.5: sand 4.5, by volume
Hydrated lime 1: gypsum gauging plaster 1.5: sand 2.3, by weight
Hydrated lime 2: portland cement 1: sand 2.5, by weight
Lime putty 1: sand 3, by volume
Gypsum neat plaster 1: sand 2, by weight

PLASTER QUANTITY ESTIMATES

The total volume of plaster required for a job is, of course, the product of the thickness of the plaster times the net area to be covered.

PLASTERING, STUCCOING AND TILE SETTING

Plaster specifications state a minimum thickness, which the plasterer must not go under, and which he should likewise exceed as little as possible, because a tendency to cracking increases with thickness. Specified minimum thickness for gypsum plaster on metal lath, wire lath, masonry/concrete walls and masonry ceilings is usually 5/8 in.; on gypsum lath it is 1/2 in.; on monolithic concrete ceilings it is 3/8 in. For interior lime plaster on metal lath (3-coat work) the specified minimum thickness is usually 7/8 in.; for exterior lime plaster on metal lath it is 1 in. For lime plaster on interior masonry walls/ceilings the minimum thickness is 5/8 in.; for exterior lime plaster on masonry it is 3/4 in. For lime plaster on interior concrete ceilings the minimum thickness is 1/16 in. to 1/8 in.; on interior walls, 5/8 in. For lime plaster on exterior concrete the minimum thickness is 3/4 in. For portland cement plaster, either interior or exterior, recommended thicknesses are 3/8 in. for each base coat (3-coat work) and 1/8 in. for the finish coat.

The YIELD for a given quantity of plaster ingredients, like the yield for a given quantity of concrete ingredients, amounts to the sum of the ABSOLUTE VOLUMES of the ingredients. The absolute volumes of typical plaster ingredients are as follows:

```
100 lbs gypsum . . . . . . . . . . .  0.69 cu ft
1 cu ft lime putty . . . . . . . . .  0.26 cu ft
100 lbs hydrated lime . . . . . .    0.64 cu ft
100 lbs sand . . . . . . . . . . . .  0.61 cu ft
94 lbs portland cement . . . .       0.48 cu ft
```

This list indicates that (for example) 94 lbs of portland cement, which has a loose volume of 1 cu ft, has an absolute volume (that is, a solid or exclusive-of-air-voids volume) of only 0.48 cu ft. Therefore, 94 lbs of portland cement contributes a volume of only 0.48 cu ft to a plaster (or concrete) mix.

The absolute volume of the last ingredient—the water—is the same as its "loose" volume: 0.13 cu ft per gallon.

Determining Yield

Suppose now that you want to determine the yield of a plaster mix containing 1 part of gypsum plaster to 2.5 parts of sand. One part of gypsum plaster is 100 lbs, with an absolute volume of 0.69 cu ft. Two and five-tenths parts of sand means 250 lbs of sand. Sand has an absolute volume of 0.61 cu ft per 100 lbs; therefore, the absolute volume of the sand is 2.5 x 0.61, or 1.52 cu ft.

The water will contribute 0.13 cu ft of volume to the mix for every gallon of water added. For approximate yield calculations, you can assume that 8 gals of water will be used for every 100 lbs of cementitious material. There are 100 lbs of gypsum plaster in question here, which means 8 gals of water. The water volume, then, will be 8 x 0.13, or 1.04 cu ft.

The yield for a 1-sack batch of this mix will be the sum of the absolute volumes, or 0.69 cu ft (for the gypsum) plus 1.52 cu ft (for the sand) plus 1.04 cu ft (for the water), or 3.25 cu ft.

Estimating Ingredient Quantities

Suppose that the plastering job is a wall with a net area of 160 sq ft, with a specified total plaster thickness of 5/8 in. and a finish coat thickness of 1/16 in. You are doing two-coat work (only a single base coat), and you want to estimate ingredient quantities for the base coat. The thickness of the base coat will be 5/8 in. minus 1/16 in., or 9/16 in., which equals about 0.046 ft. The volume of plaster required for the base coat, then, will be 160 x 0.046, or about 7.36 cu ft.

The yield for a 1-sack batch is 3.25 cu ft; therefore, the job calls for a batch with sacks to the number indicated by the value of x in the equation 1:3.25::x:7.36, or about 2.3 sacks. The number of parts of sand required equals the value of x in the equation 1:2.5::2.3:x, or 5.75 parts. There are 100 lbs of sand in a "part," and 100 lbs of gypsum in a sack. Therefore, for the base coat you will need 230 lbs of gypsum and 575 lbs of sand.

MIXING PLASTER BY HAND

Equipment for plaster mixing by hand consists of a flat, shallow-sided MIXING BOX and a hoe; the hoe usually has a perforated blade. Mixed plaster is transferred from the mixing box to a MORTAR BOARD, similar to the one used in bricklaying. Men applying plaster pick it up from the mortar board.

In hand mixing, the dry ingredients are first placed in the mixing box and thoroughly mixed until a uniform color is obtained. The pile is then coned up and troughed, and the water is mixed in much as it is in hand concrete mixing.

Mixing is continued until the materials have been thoroughly blended and proper consistency has been attained. With experience a man acquires a "feel" for proper consistency. Mixing should not be continued for more than 10 or 15 minutes after the materials have been thoroughly blended, because excessive agitation may hasten the rate of solution of the cementitious material and thereby cause accelerated set.

Finish-coat lime plaster is usually hand-mixed on a small 5 ft x 5 ft mortar board called a FINISHING BOARD. If the lime used is hydrated lime, it is first converted to lime putty by soaking in an equal amount of water for 16 hours. In mixing the plaster, the lime putty is first formed into a ring on the finishing board. Water is then poured into the ring, and the gypsum or Keene's cement is then sifted into the water to avoid lumping. The mix is allowed to stand for one minute, after which the materials are thoroughly blended. Sand, if it is to be used, is then added and mixed in.

MIXING PLASTER BY MACHINE

A plaster mixing machine (fig. 2) consists primarily of a metal DRUM containing MIXING BLADES, mounted on a chassis equipped with wheels for road towing. Mixing is accomplished either by rotation of the drum or by rotation of the blades inside the drum. Discharge into a wheelbarrow or other receptacle is usually accomplished by tilting the drum as shown in figure 2.

Figure 2.—Plaster mixing machine.

Steps in the machine mixing of gypsum plaster are as follows:

For job-mixed gypsum plaster:
1. Put in the approximate amount of water. Approximate water amounts for various gypsum-aggregate proportions and the common aggregates are as follows:

Aggregate	Gypsum-Aggregate Proportions		
	1:2	1:2.5	1:3
Sand	6.8 gals	7.4 gals	8.2 gals
Perlite	7.7 gals	8.5 gals	9.1 gals
Vermiculite	9.0 gals	10.0 gals	10.1 gals

2. If sand is used, add approximately one-half of the aggregate. If perlite or vermiculite is used, add all the aggregate.
3. Add all the cementitious material.
4. Add the remainder of the sand aggregate.
5. Mix to required consistency, adding more water IF NECESSARY.

For ready-mix gypsum plaster:
1. Put in the approximate amount of water, as prescribed by manufacturer's instructions printed on the sack.
2. Add the plaster.
3. Mix to the required consistency, adding water IF NECESSARY.

For machine mixing of lime and portland cement plaster, place the dry ingredients in the drum first and mix dry until a uniform color is attained. Then add the water and mix to the required consistency. Approximate water amount is 8 gals per 100 lbs cementitious material.

It is generally recommended that the mixer be allowed to run no longer than three minutes after all materials have been added.

IV. APPLYING PLASTER

To attain complete structural integrity, a plaster layer must be uniform in thickness; also, a plane plaster surface must be flat enough to appear flat to the eye and to receive surface-applied materials (such as casings and other trim) without the appearance of noticeable spaces. Specified flatness tolerance is usually 1/8 in. in 10 ft.

PLASTERING, STUCCOING AND TILE SETTING

PLASTERING TOOLS

Steel TROWELS are used to apply, spread, and smooth plaster. The shape and size of the blade of a trowel is determined by the purpose for which the tool is used and the manner of using it.

The four common types of plastering trowels are shown in figure 3. The RECTANGULAR TROWEL, with a blade approximately 4 1/2 in. wide by 11 in. long, serves as the principal conveyor and manipulator of plaster. The POINTING trowel, 2 in. wide by about 10 in. long, is designed for use in places where the rectangular trowel won't fit. The MARGIN trowel is another smaller trowel, similar to the pointing trowel, but with a square rather than a pointed end. The ANGLE trowel is used for finishing corner angles formed by adjoining right-angle plaster surfaces.

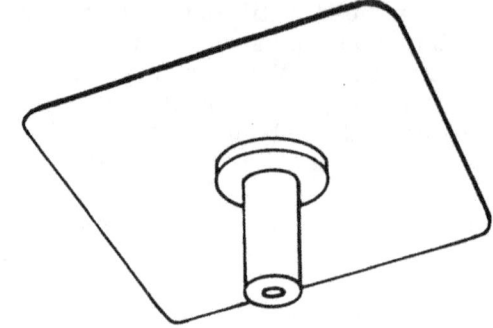

Figure 4.—Hawk.

floats are shown in figure 5. The WOOD float has a wood blade, the ANGLE float a stainless steel or aluminum blade. The SPONGE float is faced with foam rubber or plastic, intended to attain a certain surface texture. A CARPET float is similar to a sponge float, but faced with a layer of carpet material. A CORK float is faced with cork.

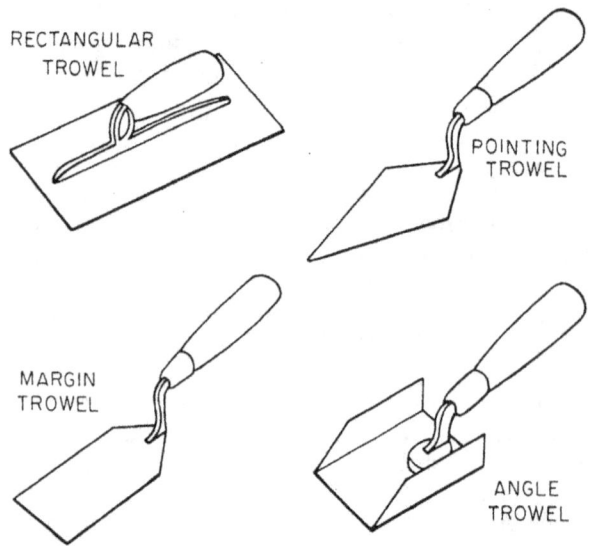

Figure 3.—Plastering trowels.

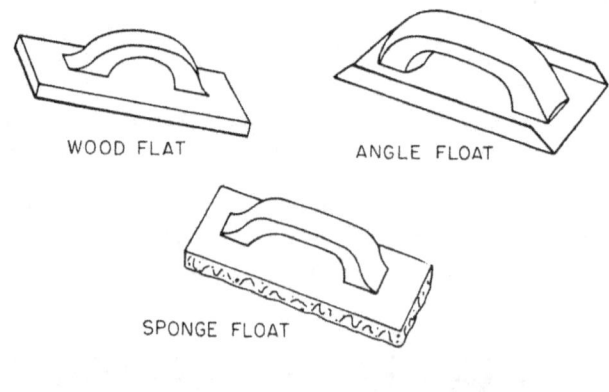

Figure 5.—Plastering floats.

The HAWK (fig. 4) is a square lightweight sheet metal platform with a vertical central handle, used for carrying mortar from mortar board to the place where it is to be applied. The plaster is then removed from the hawk with the trowel. The size of a hawk varies from 10 in. square to 14 in. square.

The FLOAT is glided over the surface of the plaster, to fill voids and hollows or to level bumps left by previous operations, and to impart a texture to the surface. Common types of

A float blade is 4 or 5 in. wide and about 10 in. long.

The ROD and STRAIGHTEDGE consists of a wood or lightweight metal blade 6 in. wide by from 4 to 8 ft long. This is the first tool used in leveling and straightening applied plaster between the grounds. A wood rod has a slot for a handle cut near the center of the blade. A metal rod usually has a shaped handle running the length of the blade. A wood rod is shown in figure 6.

The FEATHEREDGE (fig. 6) is similar to the rod, except that the blade tapers to a sharp edge. It is used to cut in corners and to

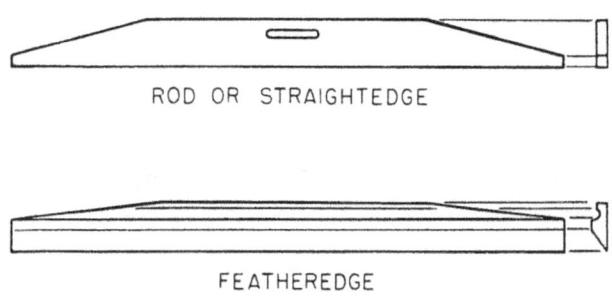

Figure 6.—Rod or straightedge and featheredge.

shape sharp, straight lines at corner lines of intersection.

The DARBY (fig. 7) is, in effect, a float with an extra-long (3 1/2 to 4 ft) blade, equipped with handles for two-handed manipulation. It is used for further straightening of the base coat after rodding is completed; also to level plaster screeds and to level finish coats. The blade of the darby is held nearly flat against the plaster surface, and in such a way that the line of the edge makes an angle of about 45° with the line of direction of the stroke.

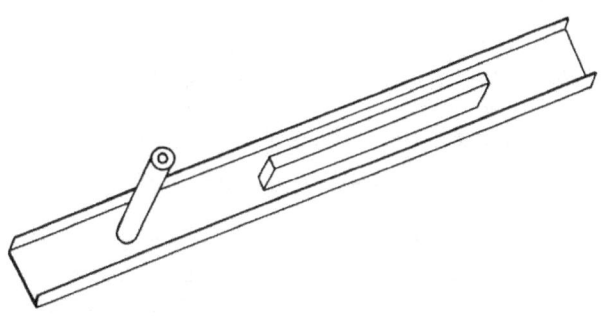

Figure 7.—Darby.

When a plaster surface is being leveled, the leveling tool must move over the plaster smoothly. If the surface is too dry, lubrication must be provided by moistening. In base coat operations this is accomplished by dashing or brushing water on with a water-carrying brush called a BROWNING brush. This is a fine-bristled brush about 4 or 5 in. wide and 2 in. thick, with bristles about 6 in. long. For finish coat operations a FINISHING brush with softer, more pliable bristles is used.

A MECHANICAL TROWEL (often called a POWER TROWEL) is an electrically operated rotating trowel which weighs about 6 lbs and resembles a 6-bladed fan. There are usually two sets of blades, one more flexible than the other. The flexible set is used for preliminary troweling, the stiffer set for final troweling. Mechanical troweling can be done to within 1/2 in. of corner angles, leaving the angles to be finished by angle troweling.

There are two types of PLASTERING MACHINES. The WET MIX PUMP carries mixed plaster from the mixing machine to a hose nozzle. The DRY MIX machine carries dry ingredients to a mixing nozzle where water under pressure combines with the mix and provides spraying force. Most plastering machines are of the wet mix pump variety.

A wet mix pump may be of the WORM DRIVE, PISTON PUMP, or HAND HOPPER type. In a worm drive machine mixed plaster is fed into a hopper and forced through the hose to the nozzle by the screw action of a rotor and stator assembly in the neck of the machine. A machine of this type has a hopper capacity of from 3 to 5 cu ft, and can deliver from 0.5 to 2 cu ft of plaster per minute.

On a piston pump machine a hydraulic, air-operated, or mechanically operated piston supplies the force for moving the wet plaster. On a hand hopper machine the dry ingredients are placed in a hand-held hopper just above the nozzle. Hopper capacity is usually around 1/10 cu ft. These machines are used principally for applying finish plaster.

Machine application cuts down on the requirements for the use of the hawk and trowel in initial plaster application; however, the use of straightening and finishing hand tools remains about the same for machine-applied plaster.

PLASTERING CREWS

A typical plastering crew for hand application consists of a crew chief, 2 to 4 plasterers, and 2 to 4 TENDERS. The plasterers, under the crew chief's supervision, set all levels and lines and apply and finish the plaster. The tenders mix the plaster, deliver it to the plasterers, construct scaffolds, handle materials, and do cleanup tasks.

For machine application a typical crew consists of a NOZZLEMAN who applies the material, 2 or 3 plasterers leveling and finishing, and 2 or 3 tenders.

APPLICATION OF PLASTER

Lack of uniformity in the thickness of a plaster coat detracts from the structural performance of the plaster, and the thinner the coat, the smaller the permissible variation from uniformity. Specifications usually require that plaster be finished "true and even, within 1/8 in. tolerance in 10 ft, without waves, cracks, or imperfections." The standard of 1/8 in. appears to be the closest practical tolerance to which a plasterer can work by the methods commonly in use.

The importance of adhering to the recommended minimum thickness for the plaster cannot be overstressed. A plaster wall becomes more rigid as thickness over the minimum recommended increases—which means in effect that the tendency to cracking increases as thickness increases. However, tests have shown that a reduction of thickness from a recommended minimum of 1/2 in. to 3/8 in., with certain plasters, decreases cracking resistance by as much as 60 percent, while reduction to 1/4 in. decreases it as much as 82 percent.

Base Coat Application

GYPSUM BASE COATS.—The sequence of operations in three-coat gypsum plastering is as follows:

1. Install the plaster base.
2. Attach the grounds.
3. Apply the scratch coat approximately 3/16 in. thick.
4. Before the scratch coat sets, RAKE and CROSS-RAKE. This procedure consists of scratching with a tool that leaves furrows approximately 1/8 in. deep, 1/8 in. wide, and 1/2 to 3/4 in. apart. The furrows are intended to improve the bond between the scratch coat and the brown coat.
5. Allow the scratch coat to set firm and hard.
6. Apply plaster screeds if required.
7. Apply the brown coat to the depth of the screeds.
8. Using the screeds as guides, straighten the surface with a rod.
9. Fill in any hollows and rod again.
10. Level and compact the surface with a darby; then rake and cross-rake to receive the finish coat.
11. Define angles sharply with angle float and featheredge, and trim back plaster around grounds so that finish coat can be applied flush with grounds.

The two-coat method is used with gypsum plaster over a gypsum lath or a masonry base. Steps are as follows:

1. Install the base if necessary.
2. Attach the grounds and apply plaster screeds if necessary.
3. Apply the first thickness, and double back immediately with a second thickness to the depth of the screeds; because of this procedure, two-coat work is frequently called DOUBLE-BACK.

The remaining steps are similar to the last four steps discussed in three-coat work.

LIME BASE COATS.—Steps for lime base coat work are similar to the steps for gypsum work, except that for lime an additional floating is required the day after the brown coat is applied. This extra floating is required to increase the density of the slab and to fill in any cracks which may have developed because of shrinkage of the plaster. A wood float with one or two nails protruding 1/8 in. from the sole (called a DEVIL'S float) is used for the purpose.

The sequence of steps for three-coat lime plaster work over various bases is as follows:

1. Install the base if necessary, and attach the grounds.
2. Apply the scratch coat with sufficient plaster and pressure to evenly cover the plaster base and (for metal lath) provide positive keying.
3. Allow the scratch coat to become hard, but not dry, and scratch with metal scratching tool.
4. Apply plaster screeds if necessary. For interior lime plaster on metal lath grounds and screeds are usually established to provide for 7/8 in. plaster from the face of the plaster base.
5. Allow the scratch coat to dry and then apply the brown coat to the depth of the grounds.
6. Rod and darby the surface to a true plane and straighten all angles. Cut the brown coat back 1/16 in. at grounds to allow the finish coat to be plastered flush with the grounds.
7. Allow the brown coat to dry for 24 hours; then float the surface with a devil's float.

The steps for two-coat lime plaster work, usually done on a masonry base, are as follows:

1. Apply grounds and screeds. For interior work, lime plaster on masonry thickness is usually 5/8 in.; for exterior work, 3/4 in.
2. Apply a thin coat of plaster to cover evenly and form good bond with the base.
3. Using plaster of the same mix, double back and bring the plaster out to the grounds.
4. Rod and darby the surface, straighten angles, and cut the plaster back at the grounds to allow for finish coat (usually 1/16 to 1/8 in. thick).
5. After approximately 24 hours, float with devil's float.

PORTLAND CEMENT BASE COATS.—Portland cement plaster is actually cement mortar, subject to the control procedures described in the chapter on concrete. It is usually applied in three coats, the steps being the same as those described for gypsum plaster. Minimum recommended thicknesses are usually scratch coat 3/8 in., brown coat 3/8 in., finish coat 1/8 in.

Portland cement plaster should be moist cured, like concrete. The best procedure is fog-spray curing. The scratch coat should be fog-spray cured for 48 hrs, then the brown coat for the same interval. The finish coat should not be applied for at least 7 days after the brown coat; for application, it, too, should be spray-cured for 48 hrs.

Finish Coat Application

Interior plaster may be finished by troweling, floating, or spraying. Troweling gets a smooth finish, floating or spraying a finish of a desired surface texture.

LIME PUTTY-GYPSUM TROWEL FINISH.—Finish plaster made of gypsum gauging plaster and lime putty (familiarly called WHITE COAT or PUTTY COAT) is the most widely used material for smooth finish coats. A putty coat is usually applied by a team of two or more men. Steps are as follows:

1. One man applies plaster at the angles.
2. Another man follows immediately, straightening the angles with a rod or featheredge.
3. The remaining surface is covered with a SKIM coat of plaster. Pressure on the trowel must be sufficient to force the material into the rough surface of the base coat, to ensure good bond.
4. The surface is immediately doubled back to bring the finish coat to final thickness.
5. All angles are floated, with additional plaster added if required to fill hollows.
6. The remaining surface is floated, and all hollows filled. This operation is called DRAWING UP; the hollows being filled are called CAT FACES.
7. The surface is allowed to DRAW for a few minutes. As the plaster begins to set, the surface water glaze disappears and the surface becomes dull. At this point, troweling should begin. The plasterer holds the water brush in one hand and the trowel in the other, so troweling can be done immediately after water is brushed on.
8. Water is brushed on lightly and the entire surface is rapidly troweled, with enough pressure fully to compact the finish coat. The troweling operation is repeated until the plaster has set.

The sequence of steps for trowel finishes for other types of finish plaster are about the same. Gypsum finish plaster requires less troweling than white coat plaster. Regular Keene's cement requires longer troweling, but quicksetting Keene's cement requires less. Preliminary finishing of portland cement-sand is done with a wood float, after which the steel trowel is used. To avoid excessive drawing of fines to the surface, troweling of portland cement-sand should be delayed as long as possible. For the same reason, the surface must not be troweled too long.

Steps in float finishing are about the same as those described for trowel finishing, except, of course, that the final finish is obtained with the float. A surface is usually floated twice; a rough floating with a wooden float first, then final floating with rubber or carpet float. The plasterer applies brush water with one hand while the float in his other hand moves in a circular motion immediately behind the brush.

A spray finish is machine-applied. The degree of coarseness of the surface texture is controlled by the air pressure at the nozzle, the distance the nozzle is held from the surface, and the composition of the plaster mix, particularly the aggregate. A spray finish is

PLASTERING, STUCCOING AND TILE SETTING

usually applied in two thin applications. After the first coat has been applied, all depressions, holes, or irregularities are touched up by hand to prevent their showing in the final coat.

Some special interior finish textures are obtained otherwise than by floating, or by procedures used in addition to floating. A few of these are as follows:

STIPPLED FINISH.—After the finish coat has been applied, additional plaster is daubed over the surface with a stippling brush.

SPONGE FINISH.—By pressing a sponge against the surface of the finish coat, a very soft, irregular texture can be obtained.

DASH COAT FINISH.—This texture is obtained by throwing plaster onto the surface from a brush. It produces a fairly coarse finish, which can be modified by brushing the plaster with water before it sets.

TRAVERTINE FINISH.—The plaster is jabbed at random with a whisk broom, wire brush, or other tool that will form a dimpled surface. As the plaster begins to set, it is troweled intermittently to form a pattern of rough and smooth areas.

PEBBLE DASH.—This is a rough finish obtained by throwing small pebbles or crushed stone against a newly plastered surface. If necessary, a trowel is used to press the stones lightly into the plaster.

V. CERAMIC WALL TILE

Some walls, especially in bathrooms, shower rooms, galleys, corridors, and the like, are entirely or partly covered with CERAMIC TILE. The type most commonly used is 3/8-in.-thick GLAZED INTERIOR tile, mostly in 4 1/4-in. or 6-in. squares. Margins, corners, and base lines are finished with TRIMMERS of various shapes. Available shapes and sizes of trimmers are shown on a TRIMMER CHART provided by the manufacturer.

Ceramic tile can be set in a bed of TILE MORTAR, or it can be set in a TILE ADHESIVE furnished by the manufacturer.

MORTAR APPLICATION

For mortar bed setting on a wall with wooden studs, a layer of waterproof paper is first tacked to the studs, and metal lath is then nailed on over the paper. The first coat of mortar applied on a wall for setting tile is a scratch coat and the second a float, leveling, or brown coat. A scratch coat for application as a foundation coat must be not less than 1/4 inch thick and composed of 1 part cement to 3 parts sand, with the addition of 10 percent hydrated lime by volume of the cement used. While still plastic, the scratch coat is deeply scored or scratched and cross-scratched. The scratch coat should be protected and kept reasonably moist during the seasoning period. All mortar for scratch and float coats should be used within 1 hour after mixing. The retempering of partially hardened mortar will not be permitted. The scratch coat should be applied not more than 48 hours, nor less than 24 hours, before starting the setting of tile.

The float coat should be composed of 1 part cement, 1 part of hydrated lime, and 3 1/2 parts sand. It should be brought flush with screeds or temporary guide strips, so placed as to give a true and even surface at the proper distance from the finished face of the tile.

Wall tile should be thoroughly soaked in clean water before it is set. It is set by troweling a skim coat of neat portland cement mortar on the float coat, or applying a skim coat to the back of each tile unit, and immediately floating the tile into place. Joints must be straight, level, perpendicular, and of even width not exceeding 1/16 inch. Wainscots are built of full courses, which may extend to a greater or lesser height, but in no case more than 1 1/2 inches difference than the specified or figured height. Vertical joints must be maintained plumb for the entire height of the tile work.

All joints in wall tile should be grouted full with a plastic mix of neat white cement or commercial tile grout immediately after a suitable area of the tile has been set. The joints should be tooled slightly concave and the excess mortar cut off and wiped from the face of tile. Any interstices or depressions in the mortar joints after the grout has been cleaned from the surface should be roughened at once and filled to the line of the cushion edge (if applicable) before the mortar begins to harden. Tile bases or coves should be solidly backed with mortar. All joints between wall tile and plumbing or other built-in fixtures should be made with a light-colored calking compound. Immediately after the grout has had its initial set, tile wall surfaces should be given a protective coat of noncorrosive soap or other approved protection.

Application of tile in existing construction. Wall tile installed over existing and patched or new plaster surfaces in an existing building are completed as described, except that such wall tile is applied by the adhesive method.

Where wall tile is to be installed in areas subject to intermittent or continual wetting, the wall areas should be primed as recommended by the manufacturer of the adhesive used.

ADHESIVE APPLICATION

Wall tile may be installed either by the floating method or by the buttering method. In the floating method, apply the adhesive uniformly over the prepared wall surface, using quantities recommended by the adhesive manufacturer. Use a notched trowel held at the proper angle to ensure a uniformly spread coating of the proper thickness. Touch up thin or bare spots by an additional coating of adhesive. The area coated at one time should not be any larger than that recommended by the manufacturer of the adhesive. In the buttering method, daub the adhesive on the back of each tile in such amount that the adhesive, when compressed, will form a coating not less than 1/16 inch thick over 60 percent of the back of each tile.

SETTING TILE

Joints must be straight, level, plumb, and of even width not exceeding 1/16 inch. When the floating method is used, one edge of the tile is pressed firmly into the wet adhesive, the tile snapped into place in a manner to force out all air, then aligned by using a slight twisting movement. Tile should not be shoved into place. Joints must be cleaned of any excess adhesive to provide for a satisfactory grouting job. When the buttering method is used, tile is pressed firmly into place, using a "squeegee" motion to spread the daubs of adhesive. After the adhesive partially sets, but before it is completely dry, all tiles must be realigned so that faces are in same plane and joints are of proper width, with vertical joints plumb and horizontal joints level.

Wainscots are built of full courses to a uniform height. The wainscots height may be adjusted somewhat to accommodate full courses, but the adjustment should not exceed or be less than 1 1/2 inches from the top.

The adhesive should be allowed to set for 24 hours before grouting is done. Joints must be cleaned of dust, dirt, and excessive adhesive, and should be thoroughly soaked with clean water before grouting. A grout consisting of portland cement, lime, and sand, or an approved ready-mix grout may be used, but the grout should be water resistant and nonstaining.

Nonstaining calking compound should be used at all joints between built-in fixtures and tilework, and at the top of ceramic tile bases, to ensure complete waterproofing. Internal corners should be calked before corner bead is applied.

Cracked and broken tile should be replaced promptly to protect the edges of adjacent tile and to maintain waterproofing and appearance. Timely pointing of displaced joint material and spalled areas in joints is necessary to keep tiles in place.

Newly tiled surfaces should be cleaned to remove job marks and dirt. Cleaning should be done according to the tile manufacturer's recommendations to avoid damage to the glazed surfaces.

MODULAR LAYOUT OF TILE

The required number of acoustical or ceramic tiles required to cover a given area is estimated just as it is for floor tiles. For acoustical tile, a 2-man crew pattern is best, one man applying cement to the tile and moving and tending the platform, the other placing the tiles on the ceiling. The norm is an average of 250 12" x 12" tiles placed per man-day.

For ceramic tile a 2-man crew pattern is usually best, one man setting tile and the other mixing mortar, making cuts, grouting joints, and cleaning tile. The ideal construction norm is 20 4 1/4" x 4 1/4" x 3/8" units per man-hour, or about 200 units or 20 square feet per man-day and this includes the scratch coat, the brown coat, and the smooth coat of plaster.

VI. GENERAL HINTS ON STUCCOING

Stucco is the term applied to plaster whenever it is applied on the exterior of a building or structure. Stucco can be applied over wood frames or masonry structures. The material is a combination of cement or masonry cement, sand and water, and frequently a plasticizing material. Color pigments are also often used in the finish coat, which is usually a factory prepared mix. The end product has all the desirable properties of concrete. It is hard, strong, fire resistant, weather resistant, does not deteriorate after repeated wetting and drying, resists rot and fungus, and retains colors.

The material used in a stucco mix should be free of contaminants and unsound particles. Type I normal portland cement is generally used for stucco, although type II, type III, and air-entraining may be used. The plasticizing material added to the mix is hydrated lime and asbestos fibers. Mixing water should be clean. The aggregate used in cement stucco can greatly affect the quality and performance of the finished product. It should be well graded, clean, and free from loam, clay or vegetable matter, since these foreign materials prevent the cement paste from properly binding the aggregate particles together. The project specification should be followed as to the type of cement, lime, and aggregate to be used.

Metal reinforcement should be used whenever stucco is applied on the following: wood frame, steel frame, flashing, masonry or any surfaces not providing a good bond.

Stucco may be applied directly on masonry. The rough-floated base coat is approximately 3/8 inch thick. The finish coat is approximately 1/4 inch thick (see fig. 8). On open frame construction nails are driven 1/2 the length into the wood. Spacing should be 5 to 6 inches on center from the bottom. Nails should be placed at all corners and openings throughout the entire structure on the exterior, see figure 14-9. The next step is to place wire on

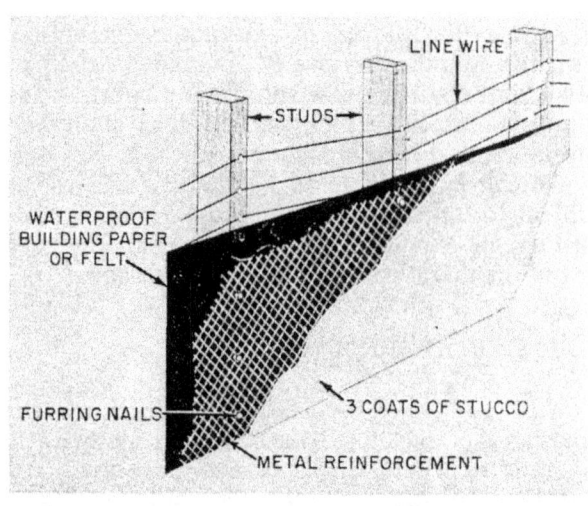

Figure 9.—Open frame construction.

the nails; this is called installing the line wire. Next, a layer of waterproof paper is applied over the line wire. Laps should be 3 to 4 inches and nailed with roofing nails. Next, install wire mesh (stucco netting) used as the reinforcement for the stucco. Furring nails are used to hold the wire away from the paper to a thickness of 3/8 of an inch. See figure 10. Stucco or sheathed form construction is the same as an open frame, except no line wire is required. The open and sheathed frame construction requires three coats of 3/8-inch scratch coat horizontally scored or scratched, a 3/8-inch brown coat, and a 1/8-inch finish coat.

PREPARATION OF BASE AND APPLICATION OF STUCCO

Stucco should be applied in three coats. The first coat is called the "scratch" coat; the second the "brown" coat; and the final coat the "finish" coat. However, on masonry where no reinforcement is used, two coats may be sufficient. Start at the top and work down the wall. This will eliminate the ball of mortar from falling on the completed work. The first "scratch" coat should be pushed through the mesh to ensure that the metal reinforcement is completely embedded for mechanical bond. The second or brown coat should be applied as soon as the scratch coat has set up enough to carry the weight of both coats (usually about 4 or 5 hours). The brown coat should be moist-cured for about 48 hours and then allowed to dry for about

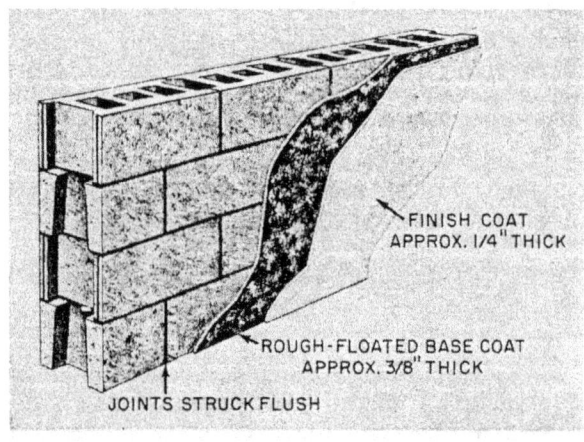

Figure 8.—Masonry (2 coat work directly applied).

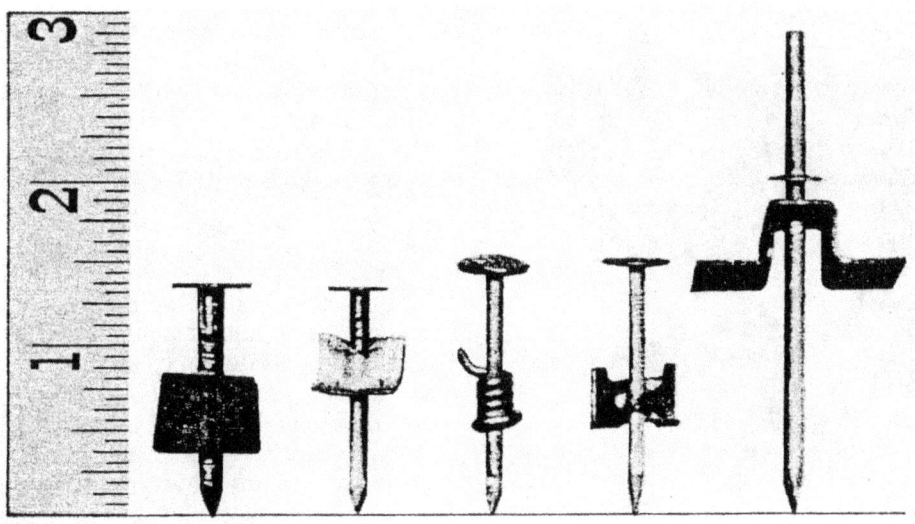

Figure 10.—Several types of furring nails.

5 days. Just prior to the application of the finish coat, the brown coat should be uniformally dampened. The third or finish coat is frequently pigmented to obtain decorative colors. Although the colors may be job mixed, a factory-prepared mix is recommended. The finish coat may be applied by hand or machine. Stucco finishes are obtainable in an unlimited variety of textures, patterns, and colors.

Before the various coats of stucco can be applied, the surfaces have to be prepared properly. Roughen the surfaces of masonry units enough to provide good mechanical key and clean off paint, oil, dust, soot, or any other material which may prevent a tight bond. Joints may be struck off flush or slightly raked. Old walls softened and disintegrated by weather action, surfaces that cannot be cleaned thoroughly (painted brick-work, etc.), and all masonry chimneys should be covered with galvanized metal reinforcement before applying the stucco. When masonry surfaces are not rough enough to provide good mechanical key, one or more of the following actions may be taken.

Old cast-in-place concrete or other masonry may be roughened with bush hammers or other suitable hand tools. Roughen at least 70 percent of the surface, with the hammer marks uniformly distributed. Wash the roughened surface free of chips and dust. Let the wall dry thoroughly.

Concrete surfaces may be roughened with an acid wash. Use a solution of one part of muriatic acid to six parts of water. First wet the wall so that the acid will act on the surface only. More than one application may be necessary. After the acid treatment, wash the wall thoroughly to remove all acid. Allow the washed wall to dry thoroughly.

Rapid roughing of masonry surfaces may be accomplished by use of a power driven machine equipped with a cylindrical cage fitted with a series of hardened steel cutters (fig. 11). The cutters are so mounted as to provide a flailing action which results in a scored pattern. After roughing, wash the wall clean of all chips and dust and let it dry.

Suction is absolutely necessary in order to attain a proper bond of stucco on concrete and masonry surfaces. It is also necessary in first and second coats so that the following coats will bond properly. Uniform suction helps to obtain a uniform color. If one part of the wall draws more moisture from the stucco than another, the finish coat may be spotty. Obtain uniform suction by dampening the wall evenly, but not soaking, before applying the stucco. The same applies to the scratch and brown coats. If the surface becomes dry in spots, dampen those areas again to restore suction. Use a fog spray for dampening.

When the masonry surface is not rough enough to ensure adequate bond for a trowel applied scratch coat, use the dash method. Acid treated surfaces usually require a dashed scratch coat. Dashing on the scratch coat aids

PLASTERING, STUCCOING AND TILE SETTING

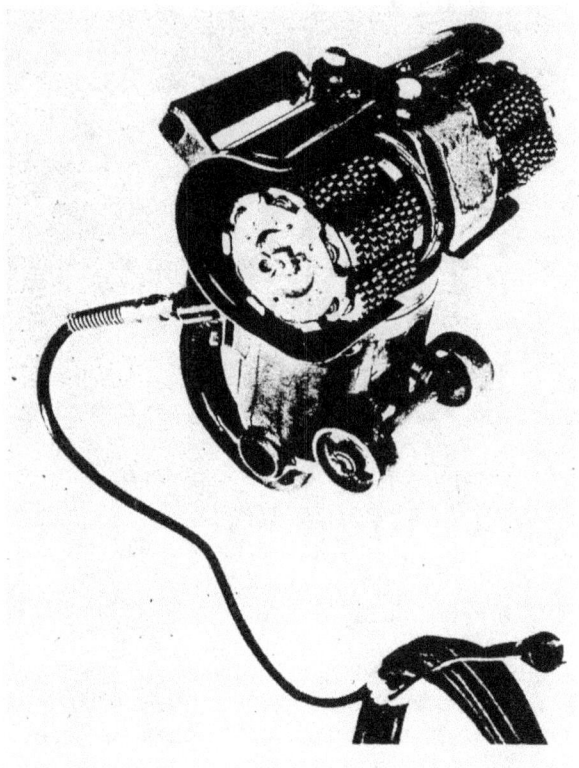

Figure 11.—Power driven roughing machine.

in getting a good bond by excluding air which might get trapped behind a trowel applied coat. Apply the dash coat with a fiber brush or whisk broom, using a strong whipping motion at right angles to the wall. A cement gun or other machine which can apply the dash coat with considerable force will produce a suitable bond. Keep the dash coat damp for at least two days immediately following its application and then allow it to dry.

Protect the finish coat against exposure to sun and wind for at least six days after application. During this time, keep the stucco moist by frequent fog-spraying.

There may be times, when the finish is not what you had expected. To help you understand the reasons for discoloration and stains in stucco, we will provide some reasons. Some of the common reasons for discoloration and stains are—

Failure to have uniform suction in either of the base coats.

Improper mixing of the finish coat materials.

Changes in materials or proportions during progress of the work.

Variations in the amount of mixing water.

Use of additional water to retemper mortar.

Corrosion and rust of flashings or other metal attachments, and failure to provide drips and washes on sills and projecting trim, often cause surface stains.

CONTROL JOINTS

Cracks can develop in stucco through many causes or combinations of causes, such as foundation settlement, shrinkage, and building movement. It is difficult to prevent cracking, but this can be largely controlled by dividing the area into rectangular panels every 20 feet by means of metal control joints. See figure 12. The control joint is also used where frame construction joins masonry construction.

Figure 12.—Control joint.

Grounds are wood strips of uniform thickness installed around all openings and other places where trim is required. They serve as a guide in bringing the stucco to a uniform thickness. Temporary wood grounds are often used in gaging the thickness of scratch and brown coats of stucco.

STUCCO SAFETY

The observance of safety rules in plastering or stuccoing cannot be over emphasized. So to help prevent accidents and harm to yourself, we strongly suggest that you observe these following safety hints.

All material in bags or bundles should be stacked, blocked, interlocked, and limited in height so that the pile is stable and secure against sliding or collapsing.

Material stored inside a building under construction should be placed not less than 6 feet from hoistways or other inside floor openings.

When material is placed or encroaches upon passageways, it should be located so as to present the least possible hazard.

Bags of cement and lime should not be stacked more than 10 bags high without set-back, unless restrained by walls of appropriate strength.

The outside row of bags should be placed with the mouths of the bags facing the center of the stack.

During unstacking, keep the entire top of the stack nearly level and maintain the necessary set-backs.

Handle paper sacks with care to prevent breaking and showering men with cement and dust.

Store lime and cement on off-the-floor platforms in dry spaces. Lime must be kept dry to prevent possible premature slaking which could cause fire.

Wear heavy gloves when handling metal lath.

Wear goggles for eye protection when handling cement and lime.

Wear shirts with closed neck and wrist bands and be sure that exposed parts of the body do not come in direct contact with lime.

Avoid wearing clothing which has become stiff and hard with cement or lime, since such clothing irritates the skin and may cause infection.

Wear goggles, gloves, and other protective clothing and equipment when handling muriatic acid.

Practice personal cleanliness and frequent washing, which are effective preventive of skin ailments.

INTERIOR FINISH

The interior finish consists mainly of the finish covering applied to the rough walls, ceilings, and floors. Other major interior finish items are the inside door frames, the doors, the window sash, and the stairs.

Interior-finish items whose function is principally ornamental are classified under the general heading of INTERIOR TRIM. Interior trim includes inside door and window casings, window stools and aprons, baseboards, and molding trim.

The usual order of construction for the interior finish is as follows:

1. Ceiling covering
2. Wall covering
3. Stairs
4. Window sash
5. Window inside casings, stools, and aprons
6. Finish flooring
7. Inside door frames and casings
8. Baseboards
9. Molding trim.

WALL AND CEILING COVERING

The two major types of wall and ceiling covering are PLASTER and DRY-WALL COVERING. Dry-wall covering is a general term applied to sheets or panels of wood, plywood, fiberboard, and the like.

PLASTER

A PLASTER wall and/or ceiling covering requires the construction of a PLASTER BASE, or surface on which the plaster can be spread and to which it will adhere. A surface of this kind was formerly constructed by nailing wooden LATHS (thin, narrow strips usually 48 in. long) to the edges of studs and joists, or to wooden FURRING STRIPS anchored to concrete or masonry walls. In modern construction, wooden lath has been almost entirely superseded by GYPSUM lath, FIBERBOARD lath and METAL lath.

Gypsum lath usually consists of 16 in. by 48 in. sheets of GYPSUM BOARD, either solid or perforated and usually squared-edged. It is applied horizontally to studs and at right angles to joists, and nailed to studs, joists, or furring strips with 1 1/8-in. flat-headed GYPSUM-LATH NAILS, 5 to each stud, joist or strip crossing.

Fiberboard lath consists of sheets of fiberboard, also usually 16 in. by 48 in. in size. It may be either square-edged or shiplap edged. It is applied in much the same manner as gypsum lath, except that 1 1/4-in. blued FIBERBOARD-LATH NAILS are used.

Metal lath consists of screen-like sheets of MESHED or RIBBED metal, usually 27 in. by 96 in. in size. To walls it is applied horizontally; to ceilings with the long dimension perpendicular to the line of the joists. It may be nailed to studs or to furring strips with regular metal-lath STAPLES, or with 8-penny nails driven part-way in and then hammered over. It may be similarly nailed to ceiling joists, or it may be tied up with wire ties to nails driven through the joists about 2 in. above the lower edges.

Before lath is applied to walls and ceilings, PLASTER GROUNDS are installed as called for in the working drawings. Plaster grounds are wood strips of the same thickness as the combined thickness of the lath and plaster. They are nailed to the framing members around doors and windows and to the studs along floor lines. They serve as a guide to the plasterers, to ensure that the plaster behind door casings, window casings, and baseboards will be of uniform and correct thickness. They also serve as nailing bases for the trim members mentioned.

Plastering is usually done in three coats, which form a combined thickness of about 5/8 in. The first coat is called the SCRATCH coat, because it is usually scored when partially set to improve the adhesion of the second coat. The second coat is called the BROWN coat, and the third the WHITE (also the SKIM or FINISH) coat. As gypsum or fiberboard lath provides the equivalent of a scratch coat, only the brown and finish coats of plaster are applied when these types of lath are used.

The basic ingredients for scratch-coat and brown-coat plaster are lime and sand. Proportions vary, but a scratch coat usually has about 1 part of lime to 2 parts of sand, by volume. The proportion of lime to sand in a brown coat is slightly smaller.

Plaster for an ordinary white coat usually consists of lime putty mixed with plaster-of-paris; a little marble dust may be included. Plaster for a high grade finish coat contains calcium sulphate instead of lime. KEENE's CEMENT is a well-known variety of calcium sulphate finish plaster. A very superior hard-finish coat can be obtained by mixing 4 parts of Keene's cement with 1 part of lime putty.

Manufacturers of plaster usually furnish instruction sheets which set forth the recommended ingredient proportions and methods of application for their products. Follow these instructions closely. The actual application of plaster, especially to ceilings, is a skill which can be acquired only through practice. Additional information on plaster work may be found in chapter 14.

DRY-WALL FINISH

DRY-WALL FINISH is a general term applied to sheets or panels of various materials used for inside-wall and ceiling covering. The most common dry-wall finishes are GYPSUM-BOARD, PLYWOOD, FIBERBOARD, and WOOD.

Gypsum Board

Gypsum board usually comes in a standard size of 4' by 8'. However, on notice it can be obtained in any length up to 16 ft. It can be applied to walls, either vertically or horizontally. A 4-ft wide sheet applied vertically to studs 16 in. O.C. will cover 3 stud spaces. Five-penny cement-coated nails should be used with 1/2-in.-thick gypsum, 4-penny nails with 3/8-in.-thick gypsum. Nails should be spaced 6 to 8 in. O.C. for walls and 5 to 7 in. O.C. for ceilings.

Nail heads should be driven about one-sixteenth inch below the face of the board; this set can be obtained by using a crowned hammer. The indentations around nails away from edges are concealed by applying JOINT CEMENT. The nail indentations along edges are concealed with a perforated fiber JOINT TAPE set in joint cement. Edges are slightly recessed to bring the tape flush with the faces. Besides concealing the nail indentations, the tape also conceals the joint.

The procedure for taping a joint is as follows:

1. Spread the joint cement along the joint with a 4- to 6-in. putty knife. Joint cement comes in powder form; the powder is mixed with water to about the consistency of putty.
2. Lay the tape against the joint and press it into the recess with the putty knife. Press until some of the joint cement is forced out through the holes in the tape.
3. Spread joint cement over the tape, and FEATHER (taper off) the outer edges.
4. Allow the cement to dry, then sand lightly. Apply a second coat, and again feather the edges.
5. Allow the cement to dry, and then sand the joint smooth.

For nail indentations away from edges, fill the indentations with cement, allow the cement to dry, and sand lightly. Apply another coat, allow to dry, and sand smooth.

Plywood

Plywood finish comes in sheets of various sizes which can be applied either vertically or horizontally. With horizontal application, lengths of stud stock called NAILERS are framed between the studs along the lines of horizontal joints. Panels can be nailed directly to studs and nailers, but a better method is to nail 2-in. furring strips to the studs and nailers and then glue and nail the panels to the strips. This method reduces joint movements caused by swelling or shrinking of the studs and nailers.

Joints between plywood panels can be finished in a variety of ways. For a tight butt joint, spread enough glue on the furring strip, stud, or nailer to provide a SQUEEZE of glue between the edges, allow the glue to dry, and then block-sand the joint smooth. Another smooth joint can be obtained by rabbeting the edges for shiplap.

Edges of panels can be smoothed and the joints left open for ornamental effect; or the edges can be beveled to form a V-groove joint when brought together; or joints can be left open and then filled with glued-in wooden splines. Outside corners between panels can be miter-joined, or the right angle between square edges at outside corners can be filled with quarter-round molding. Inside corners can be butted or mitered.

One-half inch plywood finish is nailed on with 1 1/4 in. finish nails spaced 6 in. O.C.

Fiberboard

Fiberboard wall finish comes in 2 ft by 8 ft sheets which are applied horizontally. The long edges are usually rabbeted or tongue-and-grooved for joining. Fiberboard is nailed in place with finish nails, brads, or cadmium plated fiberboard nails. Use 1 1/2-nails for 1/2-inch thick boards and 2-inch nails for 1-inch thick boards.

Fiberboard in small squares or rectangles is called TILEBOARD and each piece of tileboard is called a TILE. Common sizes are 12 inches by 12 inches, 12 inches by 24 inches, 16 inches by 16 inches, and 16 inches by 32 inches. Tiles can be nailed to studs, joists, and furring strips; usually, however, they are glued to a continuous surface of wood or plasterboard with a special type of adhesive.

STAIRS

There are many different kinds of stairs, but all have two main parts in common: the TREADS people walk on, and the STRINGERS (also called STRINGS, HORSES, and CARRIAGES) which support the treads. A very simple type of stairway, consisting only of stringers and treads, is shown in the left-hand view of figure 13-1. Treads of the type shown here are called PLANK treads, and this simple type of stairway is called a CLEAT stairway, because of the cleats attached to the stringers to support the treads.

A more finished type of stairway has the treads mounted on two or more sawtooth-edged stringers, and includes RISERS, as shown in the right-hand view of figure 13-1. The stringers

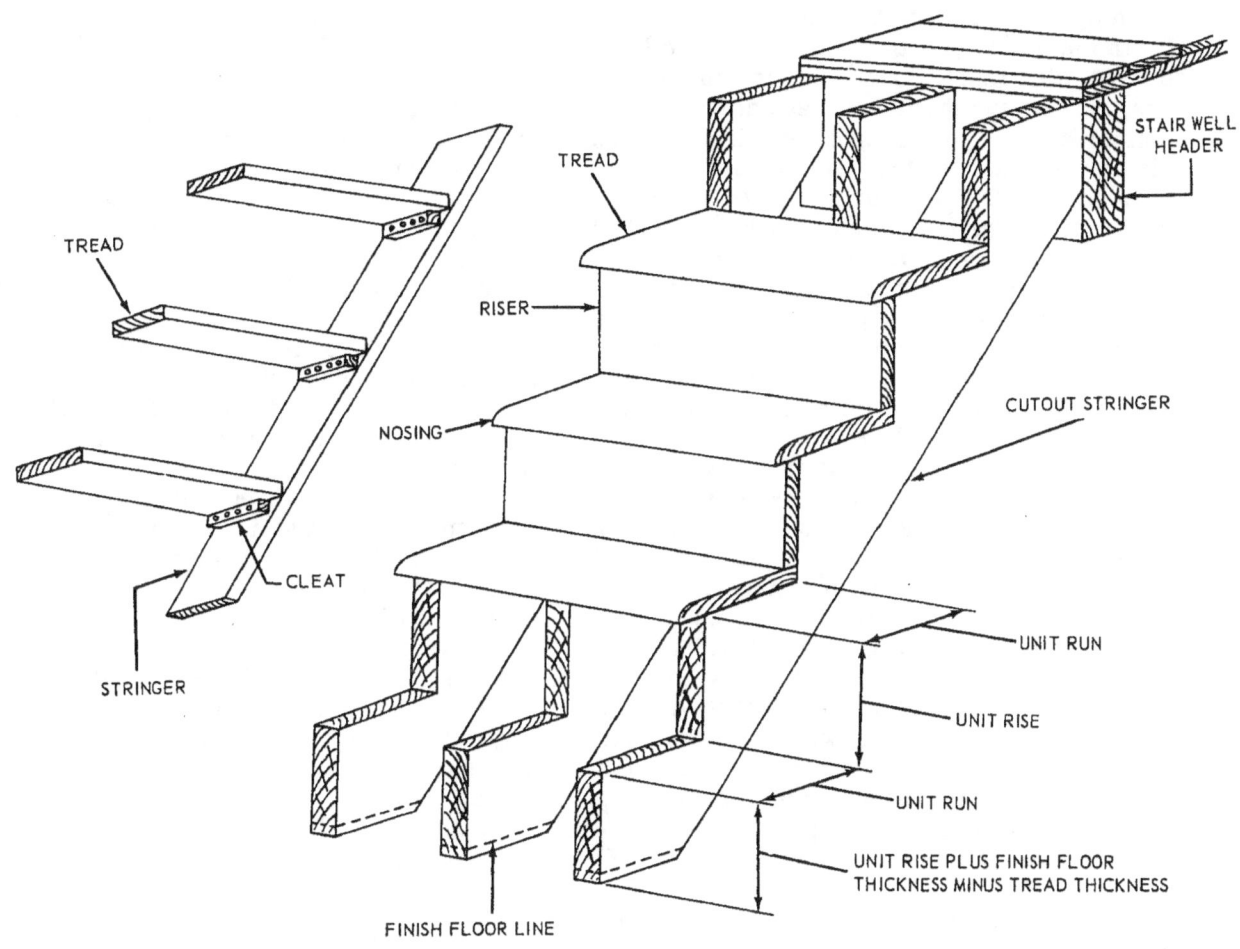

Figure 13-1.—Stairway nomenclature.

shown here are cut out of solid pieces of dimension lumber (usually 2 x 12), and are therefore called CUTOUT or SAWED stringers.

STAIRWAY LAYOUT

The first step in stairway layout is to determine the UNIT RISE and UNIT RUN shown in figure 13-1. The unit rise is calculated on the basis of the TOTAL RISE of the stairway, and the fact that the customary permissible unit rise for stairs is in the vicinity of 7 inches.

The total rise is the vertical distance between the lower finish floor level and the upper finish floor level. This may be shown in the elevations; however, since the actual vertical distance as constructed may vary slightly from what it should have been, and since it is the actual distance you are dealing with, the distance should be measured.

At the time the stairs are to be laid out, the subflooring is laid but the finish flooring isn't. If both the lower and the upper floor are to be covered with finish flooring of the same thickness, the measured vertical distance from lower subfloor surface to the upper subfloor surface will be the same as the eventual distance between the finish floor surfaces, and therefore equal to the total rise of the stairway. But if you are measuring up from a finish floor (such as a concrete basement floor, for instance), then you must add to the measured distance the thickness of the upper finish flooring to get the total rise of the stairway. If the upper and lower finish floors will be of different thicknesses, then you must add the difference in thickness to the measured distance between subfloor surfaces to get the total rise of the stairway. Use a straight piece of lumber plumbed in the stair opening with a spirit level, or a plumb bob and cord, to measure the vertical distance.

Assume that the total rise measures 8 ft 11 in., as shown in figure 13-2. Knowing this, you can determine the unit rise as follows. First, reduce the total rise to inches—in this case it comes to 107 in. Next, divide the total rise in inches by the average permissible unit rise, which is 7 in. The result, disregarding any fraction, is the number of RISERS the stairway will have—in this case it is 107/7, or 15. Now divide the total rise in inches by the number of risers—in this case, this is 107/15, which comes to 7.13 in., or, rounded off to the nearest 1/16 in., 7 1/8 in. This, then, is the unit rise, as shown in figure 13-2.

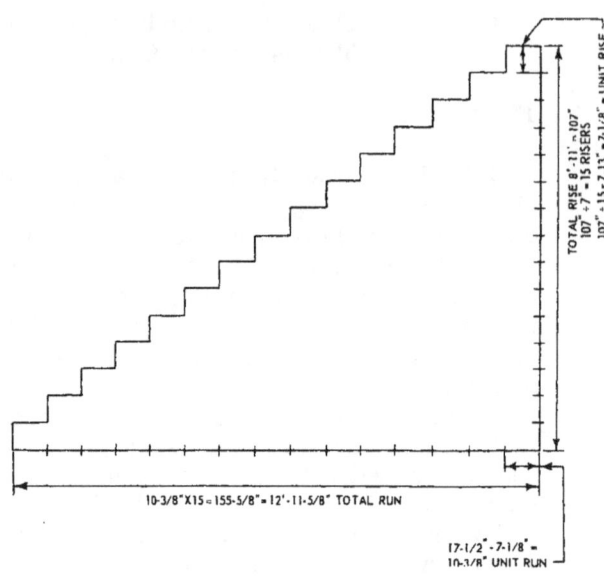

117.54
Figure 13-2.—Stairway layout computations.

The unit run is calculated on the basis of (1) the unit rise, and (2) a general architects' rule that the sum of the unit run and unit rise should be 17 1/2 in. In view of (2), if the unit rise is 7 1/8 in., the unit run is 17 1/2 in. minus 7 1/8 in., or 10 3/8 in.

You can now calculate the TOTAL RUN of the stairway. The total run is obviously equal to the product of the unit run times the total number of treads in the stairway. However, the total number of treads depends upon the manner in which the upper end of the stairway will be anchored to the header.

In figure 13-3, three methods of anchoring the upper end of a stairway are shown. In the first view there is a complete tread at the top of the stairway. This means that the number of complete treads will be the same as the number of risers. For the stairway shown in figure 13-1, there are 15 risers and 15 complete treads. Therefore, the total run of the stairway will be the product of the unit run times 15, or 10 3/8 in. x 15, or 155 5/8", or 12 ft 11 5/8 in., as shown.

In figure 13-3, second view, there is only part of a tread at the top of the stairway. If this method were used for the stairway shown in figure 13-2, the number of complete treads would be ONE LESS than the number of risers, or 14. The total run of the stairway would be the product of 14 x 10 3/8, PLUS THE RUN OF

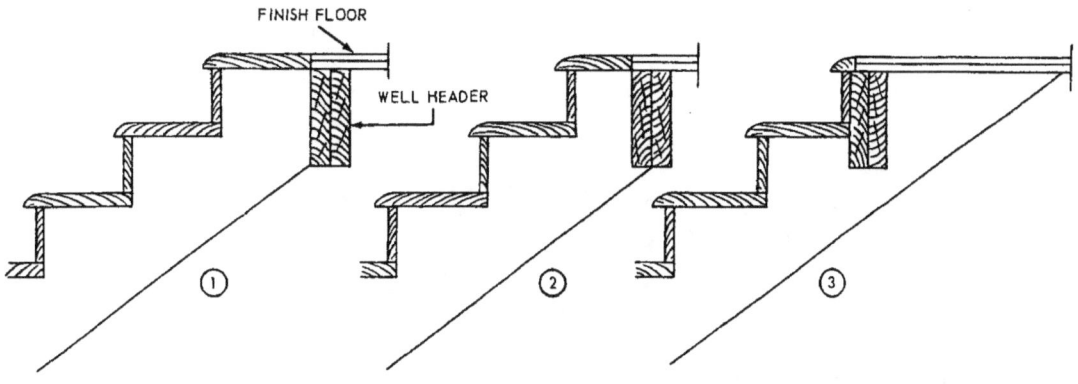

Figure 13-3.—Three methods of anchoring upper end of a stairway.

THE PARTIAL TREAD AT THE TOP. Suppose this run were 7 inches. Then the total run would be 14 x 10 3/8 + 7, or 152 1/4 in., or 12 ft 8 1/4 in.

In figure 13-3, third view, there is no tread at all at the top of the stairway; the upper finish flooring serves as the top tread. In this case the total number of complete treads is again 14, but since there is no additional partial tread, the total run of the stairway is 14 x 10 3/8, or 145 1/4 in., or 12 ft 1 1/4 in.

When you have calculated the total run of the stairway, drop a plumb bob from the well head to the floor below and measure off the total run from the plumb bob. This locates the anchoring point for the lower end of the stairway.

Cutout stringers for main stairways are usually made from 2 x 12 stock. The first question is: About how long a piece of stock will you need? Let's assume that you are to use the method of upper-end anchorage shown in the first view of figure 13-3 to lay out a stringer for the stairway shown in figure 13-2. This stairway has a total rise of 8 ft 11 in. and a total run of 12 ft 11 5/8 in. The stringer must be long enough to form the hypotenuse of a triangle with sides of those two lengths. For an approximate length estimate, call the sides 9 and 13 ft long. The length of the hypotenuse, then, will equal the square root of $9^2 + 13^2$, or the square root of 250, or about 15.8 ft, or about 15 ft 9 1/2 in.

Figure 13-4 shows the layout at the lower end of the stringer. Set the framing square to the unit run on the tongue and the unit rise on the blade, and draw the line AB. This line represents the bottom tread. Then draw AD perpendicular to AB, in length equal to the unit rise.

This line represents the bottom riser in the stairway. Now, you've probably noticed that, up to this point, the thickness of a tread in the stairway has been ignored. This thickness is now about to be accounted for, by making an allowance in the height of this first riser, a process which is called DROPPING THE STRINGER.

As you can see in figure 13-1, the unit rise is measured from the top of one tread to the top of the next for ALL RISERS EXCEPT THE BOTTOM ONE. For this one, the unit rise is measured FROM THE FINISHED FLOOR SURFACE TO THE SURFACE OF THE FIRST TREAD. If AD were cut to the unit rise, the actual rise of the first step would be the sum of the unit rise plus the thickness of a tread. Therefore, the length of AD is shortened by the thickness of a tread, as shown in figure 13-4—or by the thickness of a tread less the thickness of the finish flooring. The first is done if the stringer will rest on a finish floor, such as concrete basement floor. The second is done if the stringer will rest on subflooring.

When you have shortened AD to AE, as shown, draw EF parallel to AB. This line represents the bottom horizontal anchor-edge of the stringer. Then proceed to lay off the remaining risers and treads to the unit rise and unit run, until you have laid off 15 risers and 15 treads. Figure 13-5 shows the layout at the upper end of the stringer. The line AB represents the top—that is, the 15th—tread. BC, drawn perpendicular to AB, represents the upper vertical anchor-edge of the stringer, which will butt against the stairwell header.

111

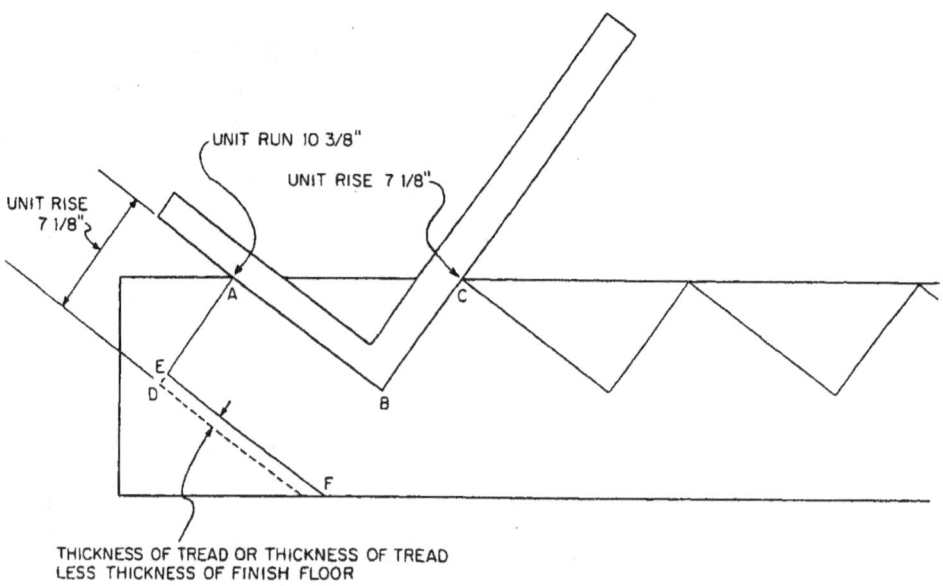

Figure 13-4.—Layout of lower end of cutout stringer.

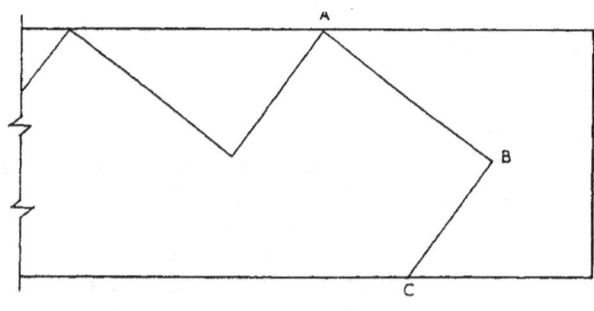

Figure 13-5.—Layout at upper end of cutout stringer.

STAIRWAY CONSTRUCTION

We have been dealing with a common STRAIGHT-FLIGHT stairway, meaning one which follows the same direction throughout. When floor space is not extensive enough to permit construction of a straight-flight stairway, a CHANGE stairway is installed—meaning, one which changes direction one or more times. The most common types of these are 90-DEGREE change and 180-DEGREE change. These are usually PLATFORM stairways—that is, successive straight-flight lengths, connecting platforms at which the direction changes 90 degrees, or doubles back 180 degrees. Such a stairway is laid out simply as a succession of straight-flight stairways.

The stairs in a structure are broadly divided into PRINCIPAL stairs and SERVICE stairs. Service stairs are porch, basement, and attic stairs. Some of these may be simple cleat stairways; others may be OPEN-RISER stairways. An open-riser stairway has treads anchored on cut-out stringers or stair-block stringers, but no risers. The lower ends of the stringers on porch, basement, and other stairs anchored on concrete are fastened with a KICK-PLATE like the one shown in figure 13-6.

A principal stairway is usually more finished in appearance. Rough cutout stringers are concealed by FINISH stringers like the one shown in figure 13-7. Treads and risers are often rabbet-joined as shown in figure 13-8. To prevent squeaking, triangular blocks may be glued into the joints, as shown in the same figure.

The vertical members which support a stairway handrail are called BALUSTERS. Figure 13-9 shows a method of joining balusters to treads. For this method, dowels shaped on the lower ends of the balusters are glued into holes bored in the treads.

Stringers should be toenailed to well headers with 10-penny nails, three to each side of the stringer. Those which face against trimmer joists should be nailed to the joist with at least three 16-penny nails apiece. At the bottom a

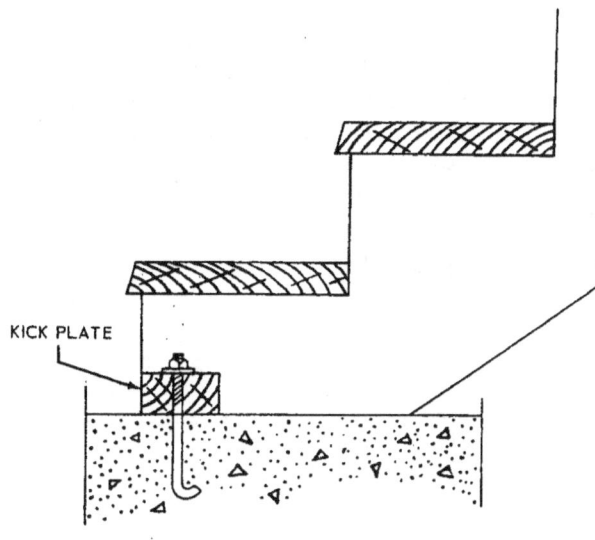

117.57

Figure 13-6.—Kick-plate for anchoring stairs to concrete.

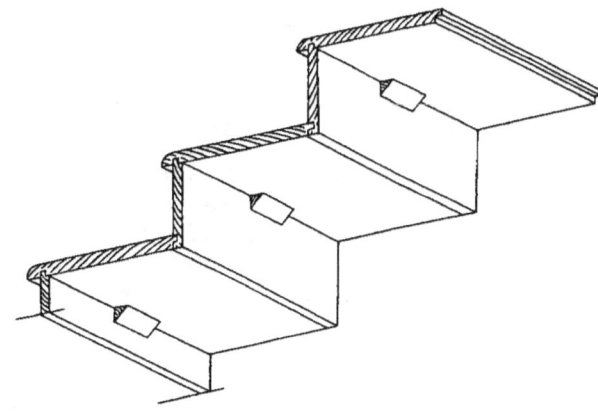

117.59

Figure 13-8.—Rabbet-joined treads and risers.

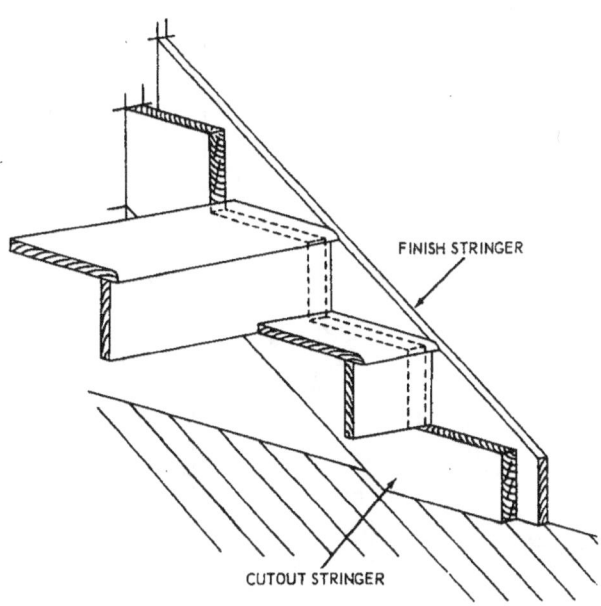

117.58

Figure 13-7.—Finish stringer.

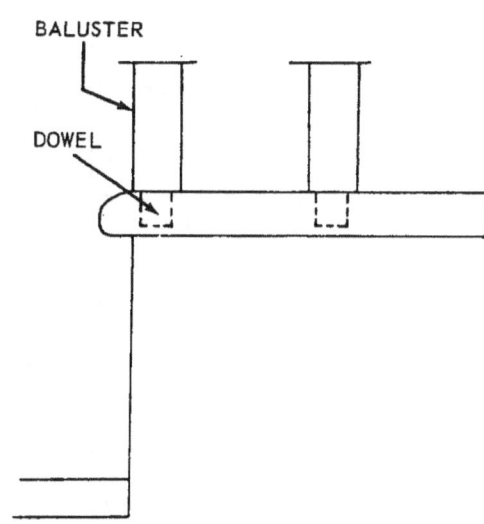

117.60.1

Figure 13-9.—One method of joining a baluster to the tread.

stringer should be toenailed with 10-penny nails, 4 to each side, driven into the subflooring and if possible into a joist below.

Treads and risers should be nailed to stringers with 6-penny, 8-penny, or 10-penny finish nails, depending on the thickness of the stock.

WINDOW SASH

A window frame is built to the dimensions of the window, as given on the window schedule. To prevent the sash from binding in the frame, it is necessary to apply a CLEARANCE ALLOWANCE when laying out the sash. Sash for a double-hung window is made 1/8 in. narrower and 1/16 in. shorter than the finished opening size; sash for wooden casements is made 1/8 in. narrower and 1/32 in. shorter than the opening size. Wooden sash is usually made from 1 3/8-in.-thick stock.

INSTALLING WINDOW SASH

Casement sash is hung in about the same manner that a door is hung.

Double-hung sash consists of an upper and a lower sash, each of which can be slid up and down in a separate vertical runway. The upper sash slides in the outer runway, the lower sash in the inner runway. The inner side of the outer runway is formed by the parting stop, the outer side by the blind stop, or by a SIDE STOP nailed to the faces of the jambs. The outer side of the inner runway is formed by the parting stop, the inner side by a side stop nailed to the faces of the side jambs. All this is shown in figures 13-10 and 13-11.

The weight of a double-hung sash may be counterbalanced by a couple of SASH WEIGHTS,

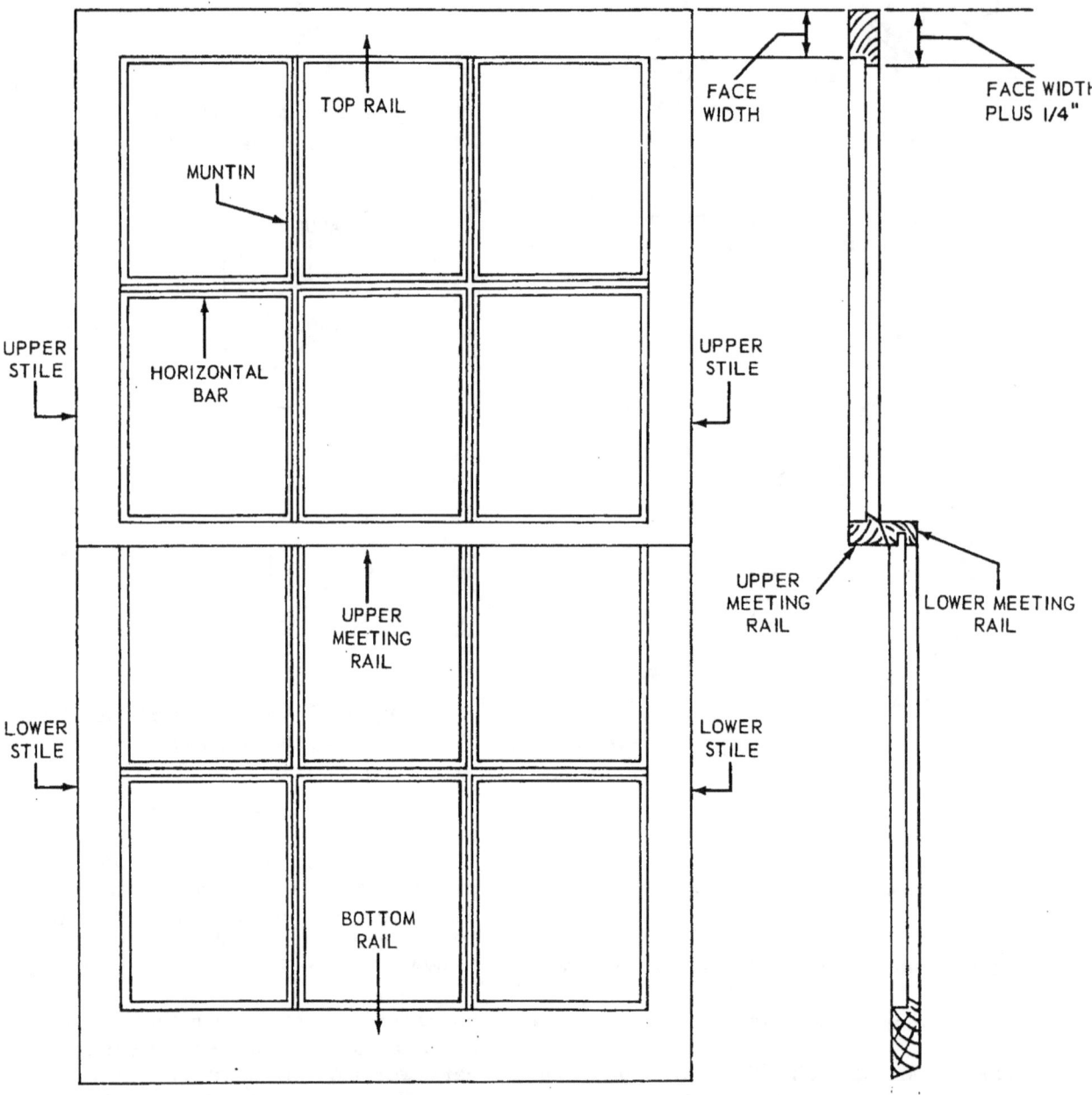

Figure 13-10.—Parts of a double-hung window sash.

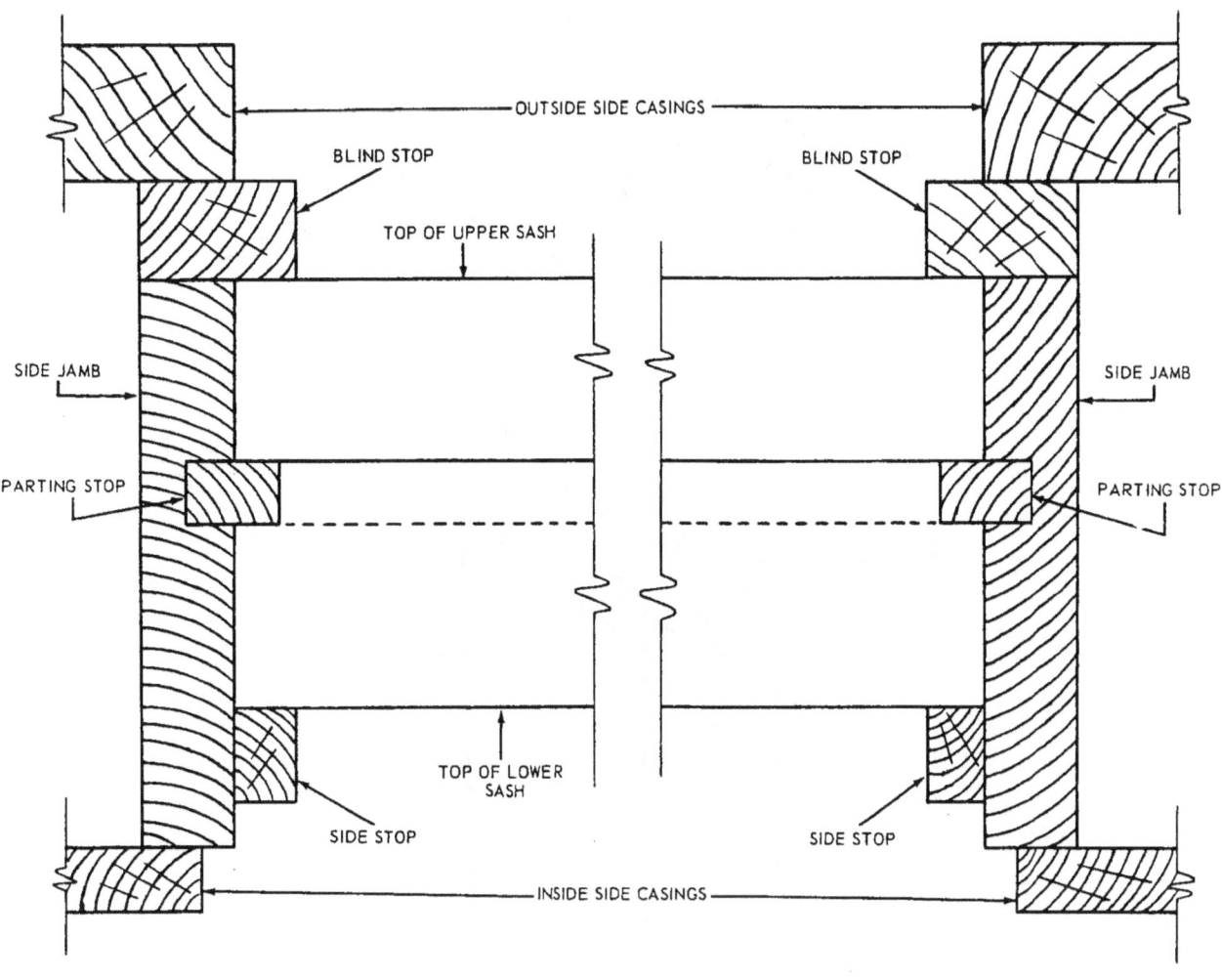

Figure 13-11.—Double-hung sash installed.

which hang in PULLEY POCKETS on either side of the frame, and which are connected to the tops of the upper and lower sash by lengths of SASH CORD running up and over pulleys at the top of the frame. SASH WEIGHTS HAVE BEEN LARGELY REPLACED, HOWEVER, BY VARIOUS SPRING DEVICES WHICH LIE INSIDE THE JAMBS AND DO NOT REQUIRE PULLEY POCKETS. For sash cord the outer edges of the stiles must be grooved about one-third of the way down from the top, and a hole must be cut at the end of each groove to contain a knot in the end of the cord. For some types of spring balances the stiles are not grooved; other types require a groove the full length of the stile.

Steps in fitting and hanging double-hung sash are as follows:

1. Try the upper sash in the frame for a fit; if necessary, plane down the stiles to get a clearance of 1/8 in.

2. Notch the ends of the meeting rails so the rails will fit around the parting stop as shown in figure 13-12. The depth of the notch is equal to the thickness of the parting stop, plus a 1/16-in. allowance for clearance. The width of the notch is the width of the parting stop, less the depth of the parting stop groove, plus a 1/16-in. allowance for clearance.

3. Remove the parting stop from the jambs, set the upper sash in its runway, and replace the parting stop. Run the upper sash all the way up and fasten it there with a nail tacked into each of the side jambs.

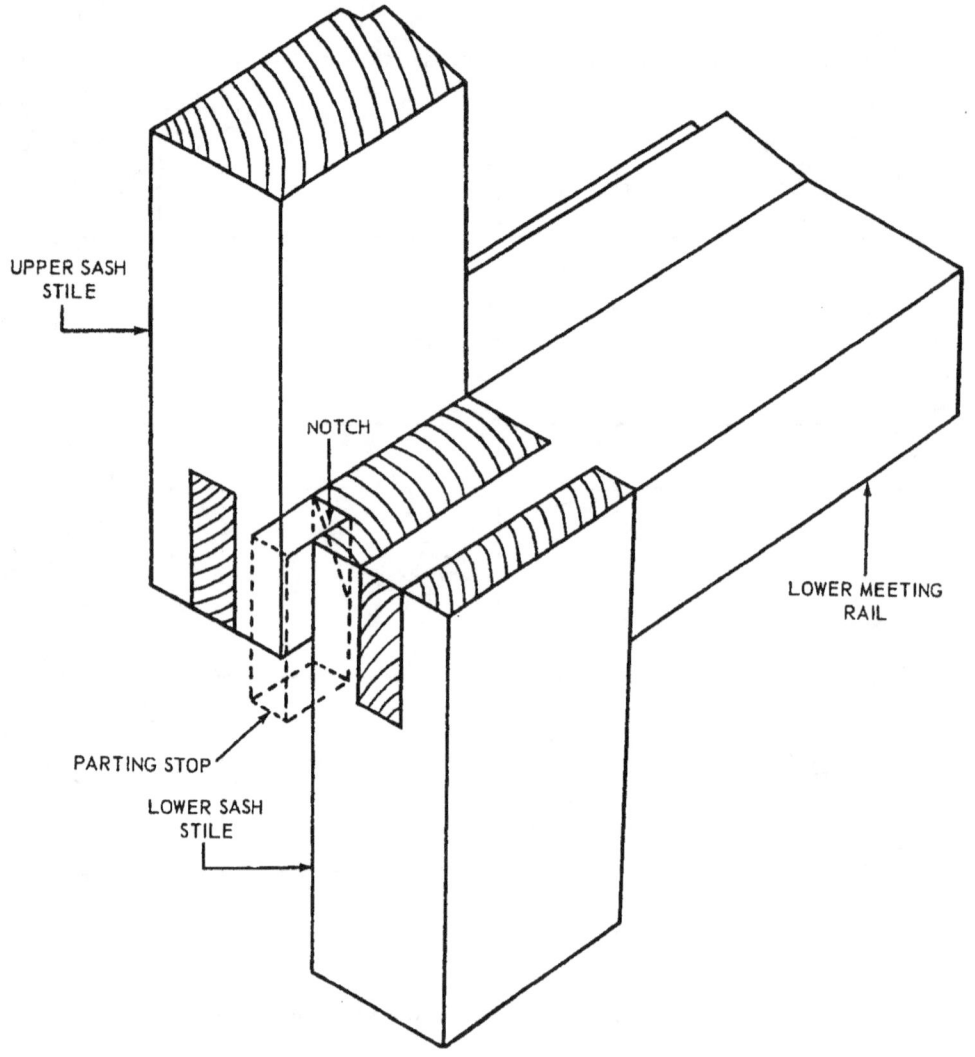

Figure 13-12.—Notching meeting rails for parting stop.

4. Try the lower sash for a fit, planing down the stiles as necessary.

5. Set the angle of the sill on the T-bevel by lining the handle of the bevel up with the parting stop and the blade with the sill. Lay off this angle on the bottom of the bottom rail and bevel the bottom of the rail to the angle.

6. Set the lower sash in its runway, all the way down, and measure the amount that the tops of the meeting rails are out of flush with each other. This is the amount that must be planed off the bottom rail to ensure that the meeting rails will be exactly flush when the window is closed. Plane down the bottom rail until the meeting rails come flush.

7. Remove the sash and the parting stop, and install or attach the counterbalance for the upper sash. Manufacturer's instructions for installing are usually included with SPRING BALANCES. To attach a sash weight, first run the end of the sash cord over the pulley into the sashweight pocket. Place the weight in the pocket and bend the cord to it with a round turn and two half-hitches through the eye of the weight. Set the sash in its runway, all the way down, and haul down on the sash cord until the weight is up to the pulley. Bring the cord against the stile, and cut it off about 4 in. below the hole at the end of the groove in the stile. This 4 in. is about the amount required to tie a figure-of-eight knot to set in the hole at the end of the groove.

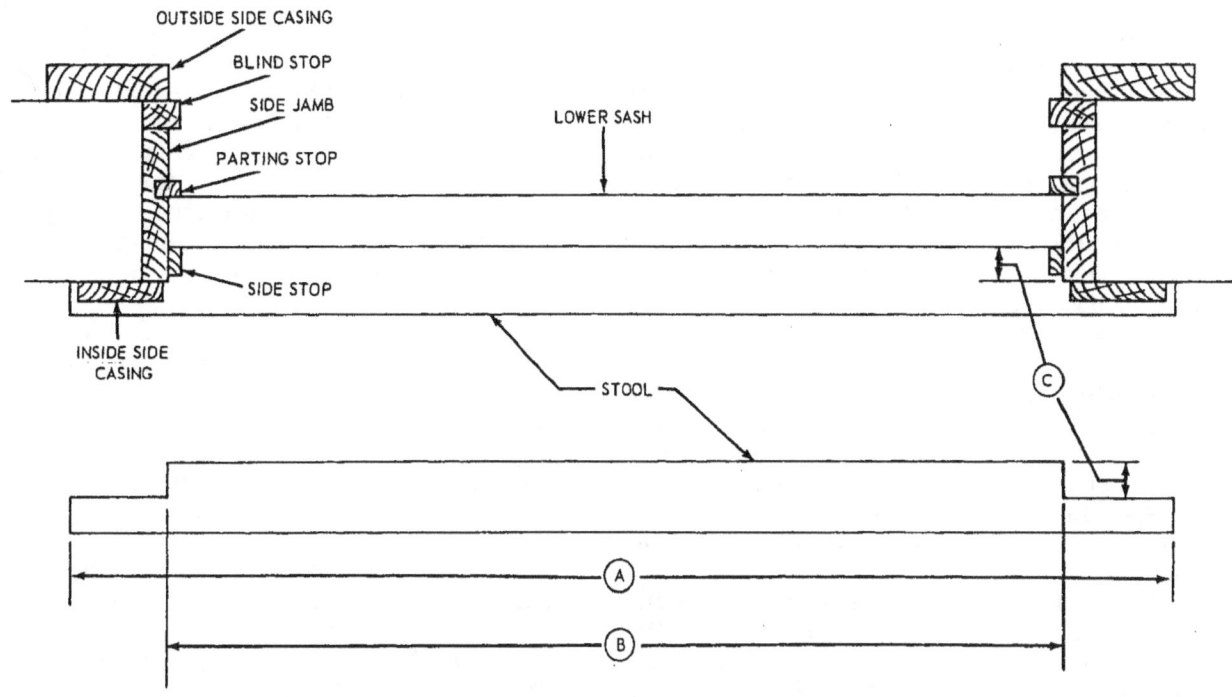

Figure 13-13.—Window stool layout.

When the counterbalances have all been prepared, set the upper sash in its runway, all the way up, and nail the parting stop into its groove with 8-penny finish nails spaced 12 in. O.C.

The side stop and the inside casings cannot be installed until after the STOOL and APRON have been installed. Figure 13-13 shows the general layout of a window stool; whereas figure 13-14 shows the assembled window stool and apron.

METAL WINDOWS

Either aluminum or steel windows will most likely be installed in a permanent type of building. Information on construction requirements and pointers on installing metal windows are given below.

Regardless of the type of window used, it should be of the size, combination, and type indicated or specified. Windows should be constructed to produce the results specified and to assure a neat appearance. Permanent joints should be formed by welding or by mechanical fastenings, as specified for each type window.

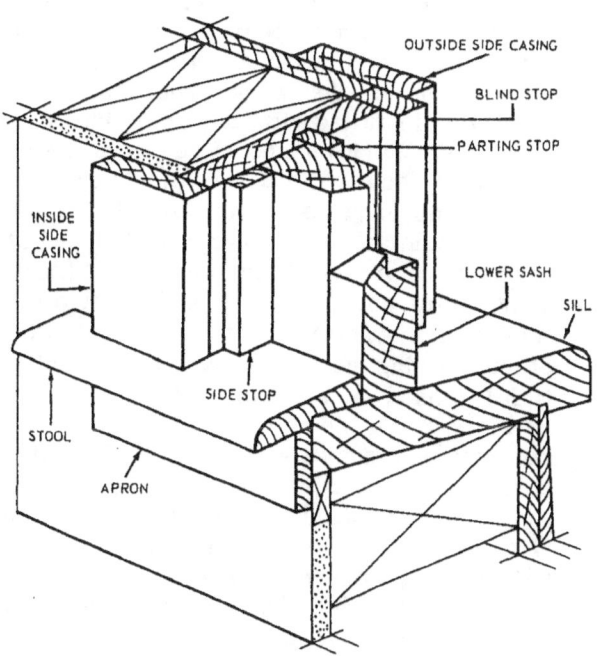

Figure 13-14.—Window stool and apron.

117

Joints should be of sufficient strength to maintain the structural value of members connected. Welded joints should be solid, have excess metal removed, and be dressed smooth on exposed and contact surfaces. The dressing should be done so that no discoloration or roughness will show after finishing. Joints formed with mechanical fastenings should be closely fitted and made permanently watertight. Frames and sash, including ventilators, come assembled as a unit with hardware unattached.

Hardware should be of suitable design and should have sufficient strength to perform the function for which it is used. It should be attached securely to the windows with noncorrosive bolts or machine screws; sheet metal screws should not be used. Where fixed screens are specified, the hardware should be especially adapted to permit satisfactory operation of ventilators.

Make sure you exercise care in handling windows to avoid dropping them. In addition, store windows upright on pieces of lumber to keep them off the ground, and cover them thoroughly to protect them from the elements.

Windows should be installed and adjusted by experienced and qualified Builders. Aluminum windows in concrete or masonry walls should be set in prepared openings. Unless indicated or specified otherwise, all other windows should be built-in as the work progresses, or they should be installed without forcing into prepared openings. Windows should be set at the proper elevation, location, and reveal. They should be set plumb, square, level, and in alignment. They should also be braced, strutted, and stayed properly to prevent distortion and misalignment. Ventilators and operating parts should be protected against accumulation of cement, lime, and other building materials, by keeping ventilators tightly closed and wired fast to the frame. Screws or bolts in sill members, joints at mullions, and contacts of windows with sills, built-in fins, or subframes should be bedded in mastic sealant of a type recommended by the window manufacturer. Windows should be installed in a manner that will prevent entrance of water.

Ample provision should be made for securing units to each other, to masonry, or to other adjoining or adjacent construction. Windows that are to be installed in direct contact with masonry must have head and jamb members designed to enter into masonry not less than 7/16 inch. Where windows are set in prepared masonry openings, the necessary anchorage or fins should be placed during progress of wall construction. Anchors and fastenings should be built into, anchored, or bolted to the jambs of openings, and should be fastened securely to the windows or frames and to the adjoining construction. Unless indicated otherwise, anchors should be spaced not more than 18 inches apart on jambs and sills. Anchors and fastenings should have sufficient strength to hold the member firmly in position.

After windows have been installed and upon completion of glazing and painting, all ventilators and hardware should be adjusted to operate smoothly and to be weathertight when ventilators are closed and locked. Hardware and parts should be lubricated as necessary. Adjustments and tests should be as follows:

(a) Double-hung windows should have balances adjusted to proper tension, and guides waxed or lubricated.

(b) Casements equipped with rotary operators should be adjusted so that the top of the ventilator makes contact with the frame approximately 1/4 inch in advance of the bottom.

(c) Casements equipped with friction hinges, or friction holders, should be adjusted to proper tension.

(d) Projected sash should have arms or slides lubricated and adjusted to proper tension.

(e) Awning windows should have arms to ventilators adjusted so that the bottom edge of each ventilator makes continuous initial contact with frames when closed.

(f) Where windows are weatherstripped, the weatherstripping should make weathertight contact with frames when ventilators are closed and locked. The weatherstripping should not cause binding of sash, or prevent closing and locking of the ventilator.

After adjustment, all non-weatherstripped steel and aluminum windows, except security and commercial projected steel windows, should comply with prescribed feeler gage tests. Windows failing to comply with the tests should be removed and replaced with new windows, or should be corrected and restored to approved condition meeting the required tests. When ventilators are closed and locked, the metal-to-metal contacts between ventilators and their frames should conform to the following requirements:

Whenever conducting the feeler gage test on SIDE-HUNG VENTILATORS, the Builder should remember that it should not be possible to freely insert a steel feeler gage, 2 inches wide by 0.031 inch thick, at any point between the outside contacts of ventilator and frame; nor to freely insert a similar feeler gage, 0.020 inch thick, between more than 40 percent of such contacts.

Remember that for PROJECTED-OUT HORIZONTAL VENTILATORS, it should not be possible to freely insert a steel feeler gage, 2 inches wide by 0.031 inch thick, between the top rail inside contacts, or between the bottom and side rail outside contacts; nor to freely insert a similar feeler gage, 0.020 inch thick, between more than 40 percent of such contacts.

For PROJECTED-IN HORIZONTAL VENTILATORS, it should not be possible to freely insert a steel feeler gage, 2 inches wide by 0.031 inch thick, between the bottom rail outside contacts, or between the top and side rail inside contacts; nor to freely insert a similar feeler gage, 0.020 inch thick, between more than 40 percent of such contacts.

GLAZING

Glazing wood and metal sashes and doors consists of sash conditioning and placement of glass. Maintenance often involves only replacement of loose, deteriorated, or missing putty. When replacing glazing items in buildings and structures, use the same type materials as were used in the original work. Use replacement materials of improved quality only when justified by obvious inadequacy of the materials that have failed or by planned future utilization of the building or structure.

Wood sash may be glazed at the factory or on the job. In some instances it will reduce breakage and labor costs to have glazing done at the job site after sash is fitted. When a large number of stock-size wood sash are used, it is generally cheaper to have glazing done at the factory.

Steel sash are generally furnished open and glazing is performed on the job.

Cost of material varies with the size and kind of glass and whether glass is bedded in putty and face puttied, face puttied only, or set with wood or metal beads.

TYPES OF GLASS

Single strength glass is approximately 1/10 inch thick and used for small areas, never to exceed 400 square inches. Double strength glass is approximately .133 thick and is used where high wind resistance is necessary. Window glass comes in three grades, (AA) or superior grade, (A) or very good, and (B) for general or utility grade.

Heavy sheet glass comes in various thicknesses from 3/16 inch to 1/4 inch and in sheet sizes up to 76 inches x 120 inches. Sheet glass is sometimes used for windows but is usually used for greenhouses. It is slightly wavy and may cause a slight distortion of images viewed through it.

Plate glass is manufactured in a continuous ribbon and cut into large sheets. Plate glass is ground and polished for high quality. It comes in thicknesses from 1/8 inch to 1 1/4 inches and is usually used for large windows, such as store fronts.

Tempered glass is glass that has been reheated to just below its melting point and suddenly cooled by oil bath method.

By cooling against metallic surface. Tempered glass cannot be cut or drilled after tempering and must be ordered to exact size. It will withstand heavy impacts and great pressures but if tapped near edge, will disintegrate into small pieces.

Heat strengthened glass is made of polished plate or patterned glass and is reheated and cooled to strengthen it.

It is used in curtain wall design as spandrel glazing of multistoried buildings.

Patterned glass is a rolled flat glass with an impressioned design on one or both sides.

Wire glass is a regular rolled flat glass with either a hexagonal twisted or a diamond shaped welded continuous wire mesh as near as possible in the center of the sheet. The surface may be either patterned, figured or polished.

Heat absorbing glass is usually a heavy sheet glass, 1/8 inch or 1/4 inch thick, either a bluish or greenish color, has the ability to absorb the infra-red rays from the sun. More than 35 percent of the heat is excluded.

Insulating glass units are comprised of two or more sheets of glass separated by either 3/16 inch, 1/4 inch, or 1/2 inch air space. These units are factory sealed and the captive air is hydrated at atmospheric pressure. They are made of either window glass or polished plate glass. Special units may be obtained of varying combinations of heat absorbing, laminated patterned or tempered glass.

Glare reducing glass is available in double strength, in panes up to 60 inches x 80 inches, and 3/16 inch, 7/32 inch and 1/4 inch in panes up to 72 inches x 120 inches in size. It is light gray in color, gives clear vision and is also slightly heat absorbent. One-fourth inch glass will exclude about 21 percent of the sun's heat rays.

Laminated glass is comprised of two or more sheets of glass with one or more layers of transparent vinyl plastic sandwiched between the glass. An adhesive applied with heat and pressure cements the layers into one unit. The elasticity of the plastic cushions any blow against the glass, preventing sharp pieces from flying. There is also laminated glare reducing glass where the pigment in the vinyl plastic laminated provides the glare control quality.

SASH PREPARATION

Attach the sash to structure so it will withstand the design load and to comply with the specifications. Adjust, plumb and square the sash to within 1/8 inch of nominal dimensions on shop drawings. Remove all rivet, screw, bolt or nail heads, welding fillets and other projections from specified clearances. Seal all sash corners and fabrication intersections to make the sash watertight. Primer paint all sealing surfaces of wood sash and carbon steel sash. Use appropriate solvents to remove grease, lacquers and other organic protecting finishes from sealing surfaces of aluminum sash.

GLASS CUTTING

Insofar as possible, glass should be purchased and stocked in sizes that can be used without cutting. Glass of special sizes is cut in the shop. For glass sizes, measure all four sides of the sash and deduct 1/16 to 1/8 inch in the light size for irregularities in the sash. Minimum equipment required for glass cutting consists of a table, a common wood or metal T-square, and a glass cutter. The table should be about 4 feet square, with front and left-hand edges square. Mark off the surface of the table vertically and horizontally in inches. A thin coating of turpentine or kerosene on the glass line to be cut is helpful in lubricating the action of the cutter wheel. A sharp cutter must be carefully drawn only ONCE along the line of the desired cut. Additional strokes of the cutter may result in breakage.

Check dimensions related to sash openings to be sure that adequate clearances are maintained on all four sides of the perimeter. No attempt should be made to change the size of heat strengthened, tempered or doubled glazed units since any such effort will result in permanent damage. All heat absorbing glass must be clean cut. Nipping to remove flares or to reduce oversized dimensions of heat-absorbing glass is not permitted.

PREPARATION BEFORE GLAZING

Old wood sash. Clean all putty runs of broken glass fragments and glazier's points. Remove loose paint and putty by scraping. Wipe the surface clean with cloth saturated in mineral spirits or turpentine, prime the putty runs, and allow them to dry.

New wood sash. Remove dust, prime the putty runs, and allow them to dry. All new wood sash should be pressure treated for decay protection.

Old metal sash. Remove loose paint or putty by scraping. Use steel wool or sandpaper to remove rust. Clean the surfaces thoroughly with a cloth saturated in mineral spirits or turpentine. Prime bare metal and allow it to dry thoroughly.

New metal sash. Wipe the sash thoroughly with a cloth saturated in mineral spirits or turpentine to remove dust, dirt, oil, or grease. Remove rust with steel wool or sandpaper. If the sash is not already factory primed, prime it with rust-inhibitive paint and allow it to dry thoroughly.

SETTING GLASS IN WOOD AND METAL SASH

Do not glaze or reglaze exterior sash when the temperature is 40 degrees F or lower unless absolutely necessary. Sash and door members must be thoroughly cleaned of dust with a brush or cloth dampened with turpentine or mineral spirits. Lay a continuous 1/6-inch-thick bed of putty or compound in the putty run (fig. 13-15). The glazed face can be recognized as the size on which the glass was cut. If the glass has a bowed surface, it should be set with the concave side in. Wire glass is set with the twist vertical. Press the glass firmly into place so that the bed putty will fill all irregularities.

When glazing wood sash, insert two glazier's points per side for small lights and about 8 inches apart on all sides for large lights. When glazing metal sash, use the wire clips or metal glazing beads.

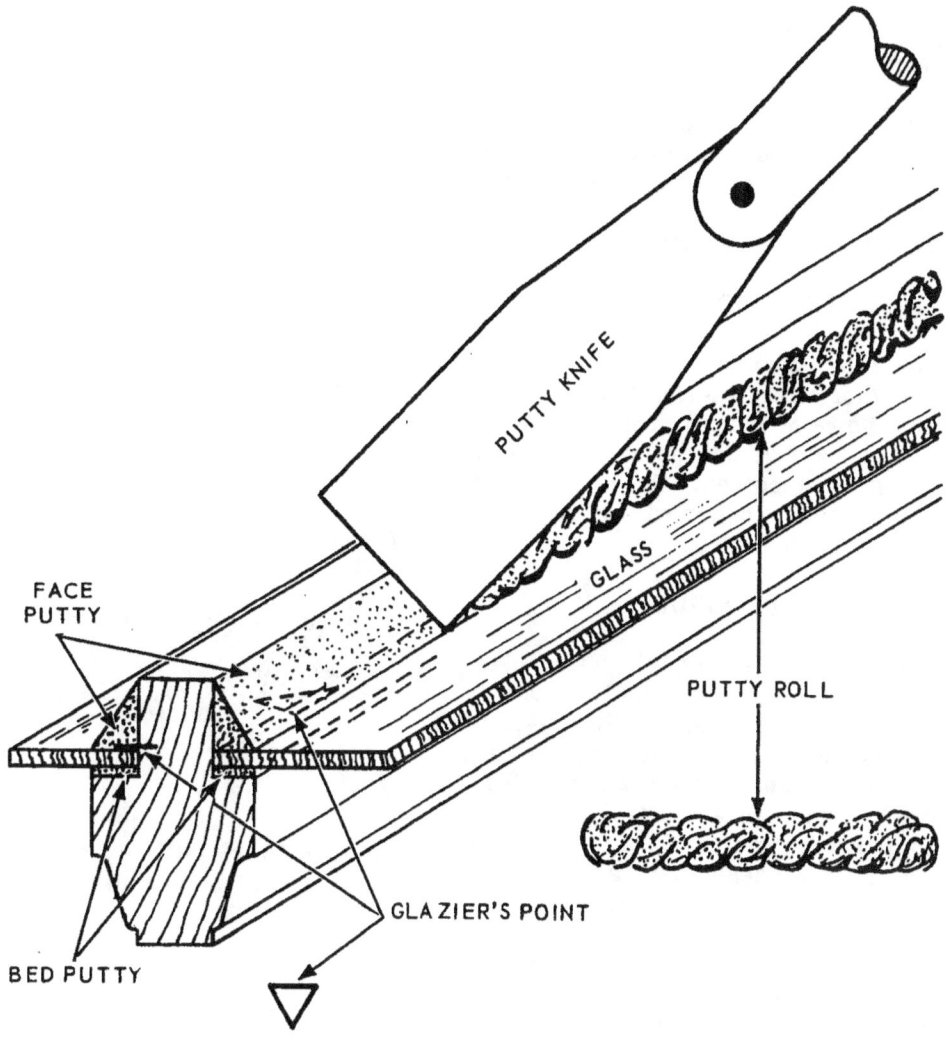

Figure 13-15.—Setting glass with glazier's points and putty.

After the glass has been bedded, lay a continuous bead of putty against the perimeter of the glass-face putty run. Press the putty with a putty knife or glazing tool with sufficient pressure to ensure its complete adhesion to the glass and sash. Finish with full, smooth, accurately formed bevels with clean cut miters. Trim up the bed putty on the reverse side of the glass. When glazing or reglazing interior sash and transoms, whether fixed or movable, and interior doors, use wood or metal glazing beads. Exterior doors and hinged transoms should have glass secured in place with inside wood or metal glazing beads bedded in putty. When setting wire glass for security purposes, set wood or metal glazing beads, secured with screws, on the side facing the area to be protected. Wood sash putty should be painted as soon as it has surface-hardened. Do not wait longer than 2 months after glazing. Metal sash, Type I, elastic compound, should be painted immediately after a firm skin forms on the surface. Depending on weather conditions, the time for skinning over may be 2 to 10 days. Type II, metal sash putty, can usually be painted within 2 weeks after placing. This putty should not be painted before it has hardened because early painting may retard the set.

Clean the glass on both sides after painting. A cloth moistened with mineral spirits will remove putty stains. Ammonia, acid solutions, or water containing caustic soaps must not be used.

When scrapers are used, care should be exercised to avoid breaking the paint seal at the putty edge.

Handling and cutting glass creates a serious cutting hazard. Appropriate gloves and other personal protective equipment must be provided and adequate procedures for the disposal of cuttings and broken glass established.

FINISH FLOORING

Before any finish flooring is laid the rough floor must be thoroughly cleaned. All plaster droppings must be removed, all protruding nailheads driven flush, and all irregularities planed down or otherwise smoothed. The rough floor should then be carefully inspected for any loose boards or other imperfections.

WOOD-STRIP FINISH FLOORING

Most wood-strip finish flooring is SIDE-MATCHED (tongue-and-grooved on the edges), and some is END-MATCHED (tongue-and-grooved on the ends) as well. Softwood flooring comes in face widths ranging from 2 1/4 to 5 in. The most widely used standard pattern of hardwood flooring has a face width of 2 1/4 in. Most wood-strip flooring is recessed on the lower face as shown in figures 13-16 and 13-17.

Wood subfloors are covered with building paper or with a layer of heavy felt before wood-strip finish flooring is applied. If the specifications call for furring strips between the subflooring and the finish flooring, the strips are nailed on top of the paper or felt. Furring strips are laid at right angles to the line of the finish flooring; they are usually spaced 12 or 16 in. O.C.

Wood-strip flooring is laid at right angles to the line of direction of the joists under the largest room on the floor. The first strip laid (which is called the STARTER strip) is laid parallel to and 5/8 in. away from the outer joist-end wall in the key room. This strip is placed with the side groove toward the wall, and face-nailed down with nails placed where they will be concealed by the SHOE MOLDING (molding placed in the angle between the baseboard and the floor) as shown in figure 13-16.

Subsequent strips are cut, fitted, and laid ahead of the nailing, about 6 or 8 courses (continuous wall-to-wall strips) at a time. A 3-man crew is convenient for wood-strip flooring, with one man cutting, the second fitting, and the third nailing. The cutter cuts strips of random

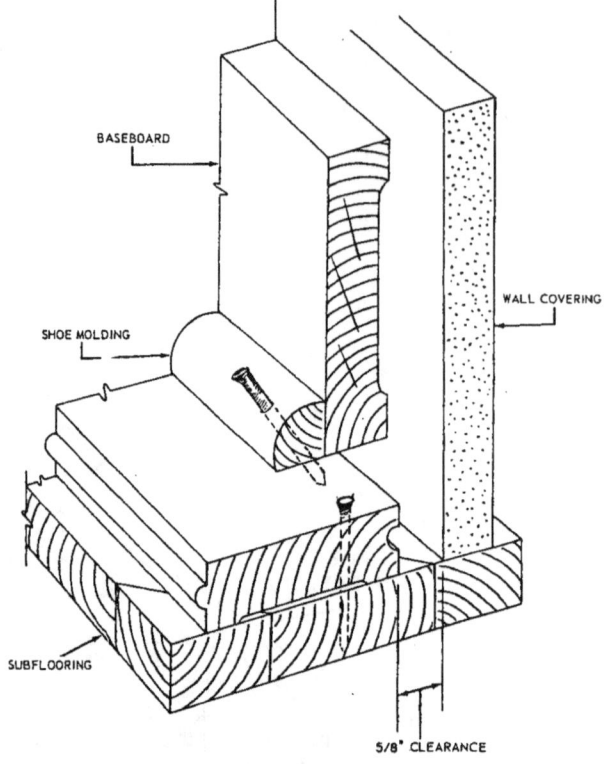

Figure 13-16.—Blind-nailing starter strip of wood finish flooring.

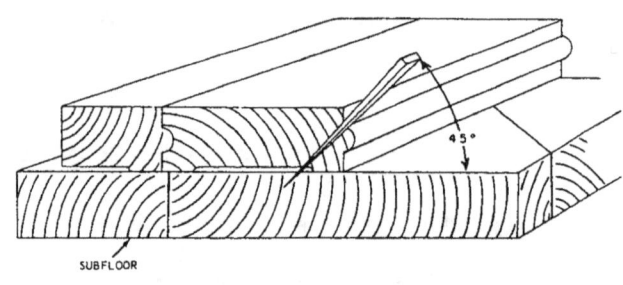

Figure 13-17.—Toenailing wood-strip flooring.

(various) lengths. The fitter lays out wall-to-wall strips, taking care to stagger end-joints in as uniform a manner as possible. The nailer drives strips up hard against previously nailed strips, using a piece of scrap flooring for the purpose, and then nails the strips down.

Courses which follow the starter course are toenailed down as shown in figure 13-17. Nails should be driven into joists, and it is a good idea to chalk-mark the lines of the joists on the building paper before the floor-laying is started. For 25/32-in.-thick flooring use 8-penny cut flooring nails; for 1/2-in.-thick flooring use 6-penny wire casing nails; for 3/8-in.-thick flooring use 4-penny wire casing nails. Drive each nail down to the point where another blow or two might cause the hammer to damage the edge of the strip; then use a nail set to drive the nail the rest of the way home. Best nailing procedure is to stand on the strip, with toes in line with the outer edge, and strike the nail from a stooping position which will bring the hammer head square against the nail.

Sanding

Power-operated sanding machines are the most satisfactory means of preparing wood floors for finishing. The operator should wear an approved respirator or dust mask while sanding. Abrasive paper, commonly called sandpaper, is made with paper of fabric backing. For machine use, a fabric-backed or fabric-reinforced paper backing is recommended. The mineral cutting agent glued to the face of the paper may be flint, garnet, or silicon carbide. Cutting surfaces are designated close coat (grits covering the entire face) or open coat (covering about half the cutting surface). Opencoat paper is recommended for sanding over materials, such as paint and varnish, that tend to clog spaces between the grits. Flint papers are made in at least 12 grades: 5/0 (very fine), 4/0, 3/0, 2/0, 0, 1/2, 1, 1 1/2, 2, 2 1/2, 3, 3 1/2 (very coarse). Flint (sand) papers having glue binders must not be stored where they will be subject to oil, moisture, or extreme heat and cold. Brittle paper can be softened by dampening the backing. The following table is a guide to sandpaper selection for floor furnishing.

Grade	Type	Use
3 1/2	Open	Preliminary roughing off of stubborn varnish, shellac, floor oil, wax, and deep penetrating filler compounds. Not to be used for cutting into wood surfaces.
3	Open	Used in place of No. 3 1/2 for surfaces of less resistance; is preferred if it does the required work.
2 1/2	Open	Preliminary roughing off of floor finishes such as shellac, wax, floor oils, alcohol stains, and lacquered surfaces. Use as followup paper for floors roughed off with No. 3 1/2.
2	Close	Use instead of No. 2 and No. 2 1/2 open coat where surface permits cutting without gumming. Closed coat should be used in preference to open coat whenever practicable.
1 1/2	Close	Use as a first paper on all new floors.
1	Open	Use as a followup for No. 2 and No. 2 1/2 in all cases.
1	Close	Use the same as No. 1 open coat to provide a smooth floor finish.
1/2	Close	Use a final finish on most floor work.
1/0 & 2/0	Close	Use as a final finish on best hardwood floor work.
3/0 & 4/0	Close	Use for finishing fine woodwork, such as furniture, and for rubbing down paint and varnish finishes.

In exceptional cases, when old floor finishes cannot be removed by sanding or scraping with an abrasive, highly volatile liquids may be used. These liquids, as well as those used in floor finishing, include paint and varnish remover, varnish, liquid paint, and shellac, which have flashpoints as low as 40 degrees F. Finishing should be done only under expert supervision.

Sealing

Seal wood floor by sealing and waxing them in the following manner: Apply liberally a sealer of light varnish. Spread or spray it along the grain of the wood. After the sealer has dried completely, buff the floor with a floor-polishing machine, using No. 1 steelwool pads. If portions of the floor look lusterless, dry, or dead after the buffing, continue sealing and polishing until the floor surface has a uniform appearance. Apply two thin coats of water emulsion wax that conforms to Federal Specification P-W-155. Buff the wax after each application has thoroughly dried.

RESILIENT FLOORING

In construction, wood-strip flooring has been largely replaced by various types of RESILIENT flooring, most of which is applied in the form of 6 x 6-, 9 x 9-, or 12 x 12-in. squares called TILES. The types most frequently used are ASPHALT, VINYL, LINOLEUM, CORK, and RUBBER.

Manufacturers recommend that wood subfloors have an underlayment for resilient flooring, or that sheets of synthetic wood, such as plywood or tempered hardboard, be nailed over single subfloors. The subsurface must be carefully cleaned, smoothed, and inspected, and any cracks wider than 1/8 in. or holes larger than 1/4 in. must be filled. The subsurface is then covered with a felt backing, cemented down with adhesive. The tile is then laid on the felt.

Asphalt, and vinyl tile is set in an asphalt tile EMULSION, linoleum and cork tile in linoleum cement, and rubber tile in waterproof rubber cement. The manufacturer's instructions on proper methods of applying adhesive and laying tile are provided and should be carefully followed. All floors subjected to excessive moisture should be applied with a waterproof adhesive.

ASPHALT AND VINYL TILES

Asphalt tile is a blended composition of asphaltic and/or resinous binders, asbestos fibers, and inert fillers or pigments. It can be installed satisfactorily over concrete floors in direct contact with the ground without the need to completely waterproof the concrete slab. It is quiet and safe to walk on, durable, and resistant to abrasion from foot traffic and common abuses such as scuffing and cigarette burns. The tile is low in maintenance cost. Tiles are available in sizes of 4 by 4 inches, 9 by 9 inches, and 12 by 12 inches, in thicknesses of 1/8 and 3/16 inch. Tiles 9 by 9 inches are most commonly used in military construction.

Vinyl tiles are available in two types: vinyl asbestos tile, Federal Specification L-T-345, and flexible vinyl, Federal Specification L-F-450. Tiles are available in sizes of 6 by 6 inches, 9 by 9 inches, and 12 by 12 inches, and in thicknesses of 1/8 and 3/32 inch. Vinyl is also available in 54-inch sheets. Vinyl tile may be laid on a concrete floor in direct contact with the ground only if the slab is membrane-waterproofed. Vinyl tiles are durable and easy to keep clean. Vinyl plastic floorings have good resistance to abrasion, are impervious to water, and are outstanding in resistance to grease, oils, and alkalies.

Asphalt and vinyl tiles should be laid according to the manufacturer's recommendations, with or without lining felt as suitable for the application. Before the tile is laid, the floor area should be squared and the best method of laying the tile determined, depending on the shape of the room, location of fixed furnishings and equipment, and doorways. Tile should always be laid from the center of the room toward the walls so that border widths can be adjusted accordingly. Tiles should be stored for 24 hours before installation in a room heated to at least 70 degrees. Cold tiles may cause condensation on the underside and break down the cement bond. Cement should be spread at a uniform consistency ahead of the work and allowed to dry to a tacky state before tile is laid in it.

CERAMIC AND QUARRY FLOOR TILE

Ceramic floor tile is glazed or unglazed, manufactured in small square, hexagonal, rectangular, and circular shapes about 1/4 inch thick, and often arranged in mosaic patterns. The pieces are usually factory-assembled (face side up) on paper sheets in the required pattern, laid on a mortar setting bed, pressed firmly on the mortar, and tamped true and even with the finished floor line. Grout is then forced into the joints, filling them completely, and is finished flush and level with the floor line.

Quarry tile is usually unglazed and manufactured in square and rectangular shapes, ranging from 2 3/4 inches to 9 inches in width, from 2 3/4 inches to 12 inches in length, and of varying thicknesses. Tiles are laid individually on a mortar setting bed with joints about 1/2 inch wide.

In locations such as galleys and food preparation areas, where the floor is directly exposed to the effects of corrosion agents, use acid-resistant joint material to fill the joints. The acid-resistant mortars are proprietary products and should be mixed in accordance with the manufacturer's recommendations. They should be composed of powdered resin and liquid resin cement and be resistant to the effects of oils, fats, greases, organic and inorganic acids, salts, alkalies, and mineral solvents.

DOORS

Inside door frames are constructed in several ways. The interior type is constructed like the outside type except that no casing is used on inside door frames. Hinge blocks are nailed to the inside wall finish, where the hinges are to be placed, to provide a nailing surface for the hinge flush with the door. Both the outside and inside door frames may be modified to suit a climatic condition.

DOOR JAMBS

Door jambs (fig. 13-18) are the linings of the framing of door openings. Casings and stops are nailed to the door jambs and the door is hung from them. Inside jambs are made of 3/4-inch stock and outside jambs of 1 3/8-inch stock. The width of the stock will vary in accordance with the thickness of the walls. Inside jambs are built up with 3/8- by 1 3/8-inch stops nailed to the jamb, while outside jambs are usually rabbeted out to receive the door. Jambs are made and set in the following manner:

Regardless of how carefully rough openings are made, be sure to plumb the jambs and level the heads, when jambs are set.

Rough openings are usually made 2 1/2 inches larger in width and height than the size of the door to be hung. For example, a 2-foot 8-inch by 6-foot 8-inch door would need a rough opening of 2 feet 10 1/2 inches by 6 feet 10 1/2 inches. This extra space allows for the jambs, the wedging, and the clearance space for the door to swing.

Level the floor across the opening to determine any variation in floor heights at the point where the jambs rest on the floor.

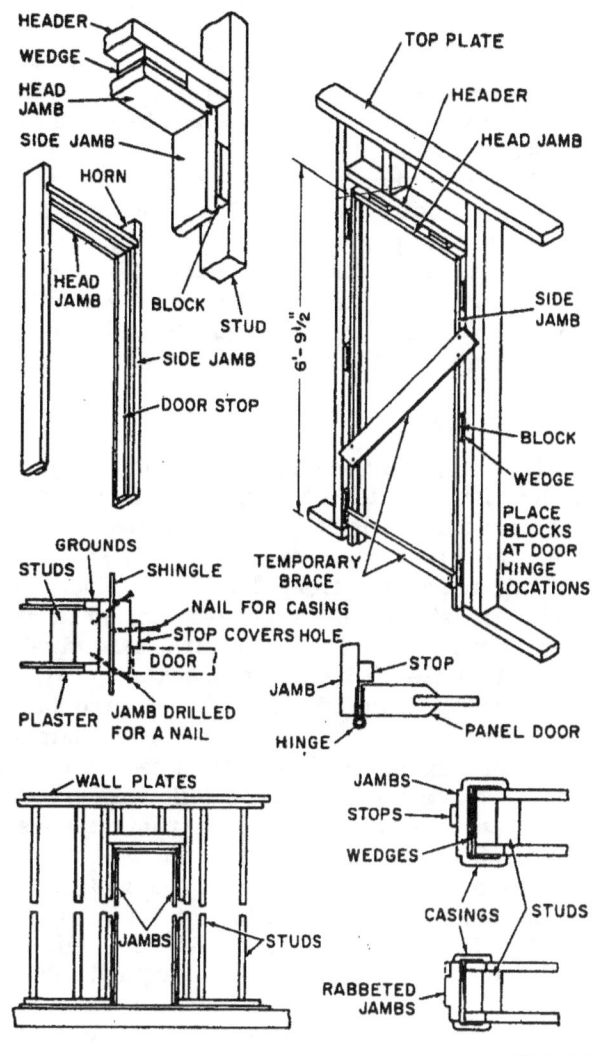

Figure 13-18.—Door jamb and door trim.

Now cut the head jamb with both ends square, having allowed width of the door plus the depth of both dadoes and a full 3/16 inch for door clearance.

From the lower edge of the dado, measure a distance equal to the height of the door plus the clearance wanted under it. Mark and cut square.

On the opposite jamb do the same, only make additions or subtractions for the variation in the floor, if any.

Now nail the jambs and jamb heads together with 8-penny common nails through the dado into the head jamb.

Set the jambs into the opening and place small blocks under each jamb on the subfloor just as thick as the finish floor will be. This is to allow the finish floor to go under.

Plumb the jambs and level the jamb head.

Wedge the sides with shingles between the jambs and the studs, to align, and then nail securely in place.

Take care not to wedge the jamb unevenly.

Use a straightedge 5 or 6 feet long inside the jambs to help prevent uneven wedging.

Check jambs and head carefully, because jambs placed out of plumb will have a tendency to swing the door open or shut, depending on the direction in which the jamb is out of plumb.

DOOR TRIM

Door trim material is nailed onto the jambs to provide a finish between the jambs and the plastered wall. It is frequently called "casing" (fig. 13-18). Sizes vary from 1/2 to 3/4 inches in thickness, and from 2 1/2 to 6 inches in width. Most trim has a concave back, to fit over uneven plaster. In mitered work, care must be taken to make all joints clean, square, neat, and well fitted. (If the trim is to be mitered at the top corners, a miter box, miter square, hammer nail set, and block plane will be needed.) Door openings are cased up in the following manner:

Leave a margin of 1/4-inch from the edge of the jamb to the casing all around.

Cut one of the side casings square and even at the bottom, with the bottom of the jamb.

Cut the top or mitered end next, allowing 1/4-inch extra length for the margin at the top.

Nail the casing onto the jamb and even with the 1/4-inch margin line, starting at the top and working toward the bottom.

Use 4-penny finish nails along the jamb side and 6-penny or 8-penny case nails along the outer edge of the casings.

The nails along the outer edge will need to be long enough to go through the casing and plaster and into the studs.

Set all nailheads about 1/8 inch below the surface of the wood with a nail set.

Now apply the casing for the other side and then the head casing.

FITTING A DOOR

If a number of doors are to be fitted and hung, a DOOR JACK like the one shown in figure 13-19 should be constructed, to hold doors upright for the planing of edges and the installation of HARDWARE (hinges, locks, knobs, and other metal fittings on a door or window).

NOTE: The edge of the door can be beveled to prevent binding and to give a tighter fit.

The first step in fitting a door is to determine from the floor plan which stile is the hinge stile and which the lock stile, and to mark both the stiles and the corresponding jambs accordingly. Next, carefully measure the height of the finished opening ON BOTH SIDE JAMBS and the width of the opening AT BOTH TOP AND BOTTOM. The finished opening should be perfectly rectangular; but IT MAY NOT BE. Your job now is to fit the door accurately to the opening, regardless of the shape of the opening.

A well-fitted door, when hung, should conform to the shape of the finished opening, less a clearance allowance of 1/16 in. at the sides and on top. For an interior door without sill or threshold there should be a bottom clearance above the finished floor of from 3/8 to 1/2 in. This clearance is required to ensure that the door will swing clear of carpeting; if the carpeting is to be extra-thick, the bottom clearance will have to be greater than 1/2 in. For a door with a sill and no threshold, the bottom clearance should be 1/16 in. above the sill. For a door with a threshold, the bottom clearance should be 1/16 above the threshold. The sill and threshold, if any, should be set in place before the door is hung.

Lay off the measured dimensions of the finished opening, less allowances, on the door. Check the door jambs for trueness, and if you find any irregularities, transfer them to the door lines. Place the door in the jack and plane the edges to the lines, setting the door in the opening frequently to check the fit.

HANGING A DOOR

You will be dealing mainly with doors equipped with SIDE hinges (hinges located on the edges of one stile or the other). There are various types of side hinges, but yours will be mostly LOOSE-PIN BUTT MORTISE hinges like the one shown in figure 13-20. A loose-pin butt hinge consists of two rectangular LEAVES, pivoted on a PIN which is called a LOOSE PIN because it can be removed by simple extraction. The hinge is called a MORTISE hinge because the leaves are MORTISED into gains cut in the hinge stile of the door and the hinge jamb of the door frame.

The first step in hanging a door is to lay out the locations of the hinges on the hinge stile and the hinge jamb. Set the door in the frame, and

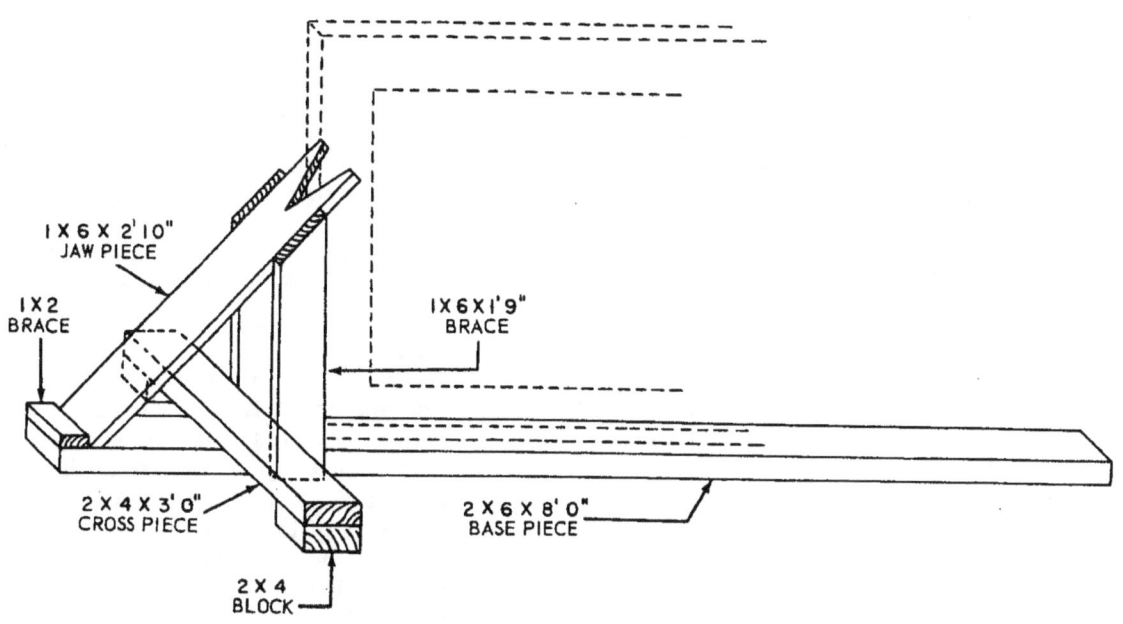

Figure 13-19.—Door jack.

117.68

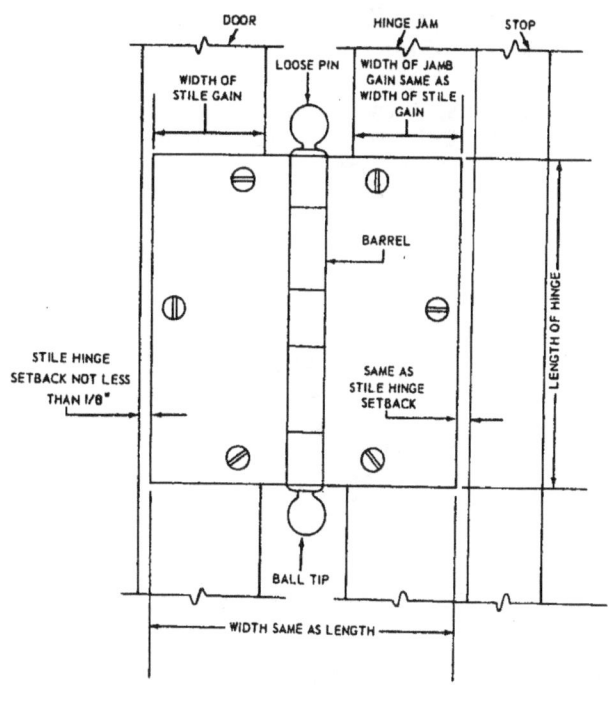

Figure 13-20.—Loose-pin butt mortise hinge.

117.69

force the hinge stile against the hinge jamb with the wedge marked A in figure 13-21. Then insert a 4-penny finish nail between the top rail and the head jamb, and force the top rail up against the nail with the wedge marked B in the figure. Since a 4-penny finish nail has a diameter of 1/16 in. (which is the standard top clearance for a door), the door is now at the correct height.

Exterior doors usually have 3 hinges, interior doors, as a rule, only 2. The vertical distance between the top of the door and the top of the top hinge, and between the top of the finish floor and the bottom of the bottom hinge, may be specified. If not, the distances customarily used are those shown in figure 13-21. The middle hinge, if there is one, is usually located midway between the other two.

The size of a loose-pin butt mortise hinge is designated by the length (height) and by the combined width of the leaves in inches (height is always given first). The width varies with the requirements of setback, clearance, door thickness, etc., and is calculated individually for each door. Doors 1 1/8 to 1 3/8 in. thick and up to 32-in. wide take a 3 1/2-in. hinge. Doors 1 1/8 to 1 3/8 in. thick and from 32 to 37-in. wide take a 4-in. hinge. Doors more than 1 3/8 in. but not more than 1 7/8 in. thick and up to 32-in. wide take a 4 1/2 in. hinge; if more than 32 but not more than 37-in. wide they take a 5-in. hinge; if from 37 to 43-in. wide they take a 5-in. EXTRA HEAVY hinge. Doors thicker than 1 7/8

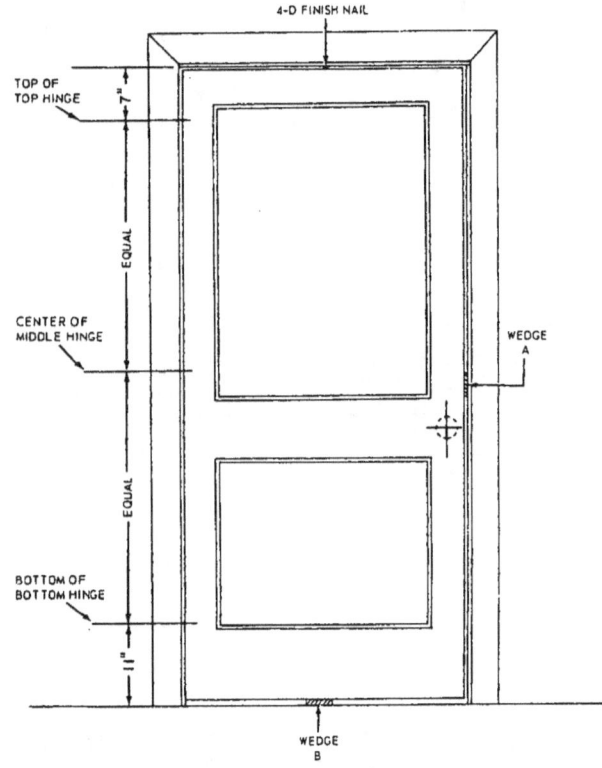

Figure 13-21.—Laying out hinge locations on a door.

the lock jamb too large, the gains are too deep. This can be corrected by shimming up the leaves with strips of cardboard placed in the gains.

INSTALLING A CYLINDER LOCK

The parts of an ordinary cylinder LOCK for a door are shown in figure 13-22. The procedure for installing a lock of this type is as follows:

Open the door to a convenient working position and check it in place with wedges under the bottom near the outer edge.

Measure up 36 in. from the floor (the usual knob height), and square a line across the face and edge of the lock stile.

Use the template that is usually supplied with cylinder lock; place the template on the face of the door (at proper height and alignment with layout lines) and mark the centers of holes to be drilled. (See fig. 13-23.)

Drill the holes through the face of the door and then the one through the edge to receive the latch bolt. It should be slightly deeper than the length of the bolt.

Cut a gain for the latch-bolt mounting plate, and install the latch unit.

Install interior and exterior knobs.

Find the position of the strike plate and install it in the jamb.

in. and up to 43-in. wide take a 5-in. extra heavy hinge. Doors thicker than 1 7/8 in. and wider than 43-in. take a 6-in. extra heavy hinge.

Place the door in the door jack and lay off the outlines of the gains on the edge of the hinge stile, using a hinge leaf as a marker. The STILE HINGE SETBACK (shown in fig. 13-20) should be not less than 1/8-in. and is usually made about 1/4-in. Lay out gains of exactly the same size on the hinge jamb, and then chisel out the gains to a depth exactly equal to the thickness of a leaf.

Separate the leaves on the hinges by extracting the loose pins, and screw the leaves into the gains, taking care to ensure that the loose pin will be up when the door is hung in place. Hang the door in place, insert the loose pins, and check the clearances at the side jambs. If the clearance along the hinge jamb is too large (more than 1/16-in.) and that along the lock jamb too small (less than 1/16), remove the door, remove the hinge leaves from the gains, and slightly deepen the gains. If the clearance along the hinge jamb is too small and that along

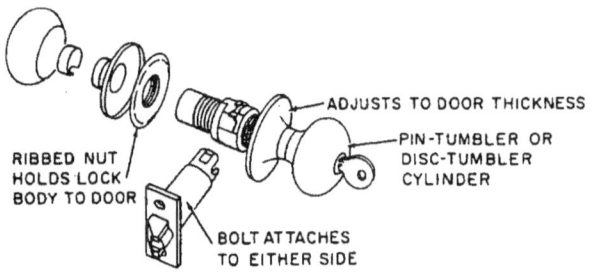

Figure 13-22.—Parts of a cylinder lock.

INTERIOR TRIM

The casing around the doors and windows, the baseboard with its base mold and shoe mold, the picture mold, chair rail, cornice mold, and panel mold are the various trim members used in finishing the interior of a building.

Various types of wood can be used for interior trim, such as birch, oak, mahogany, walnut, white and yellow pine, and other available woods.

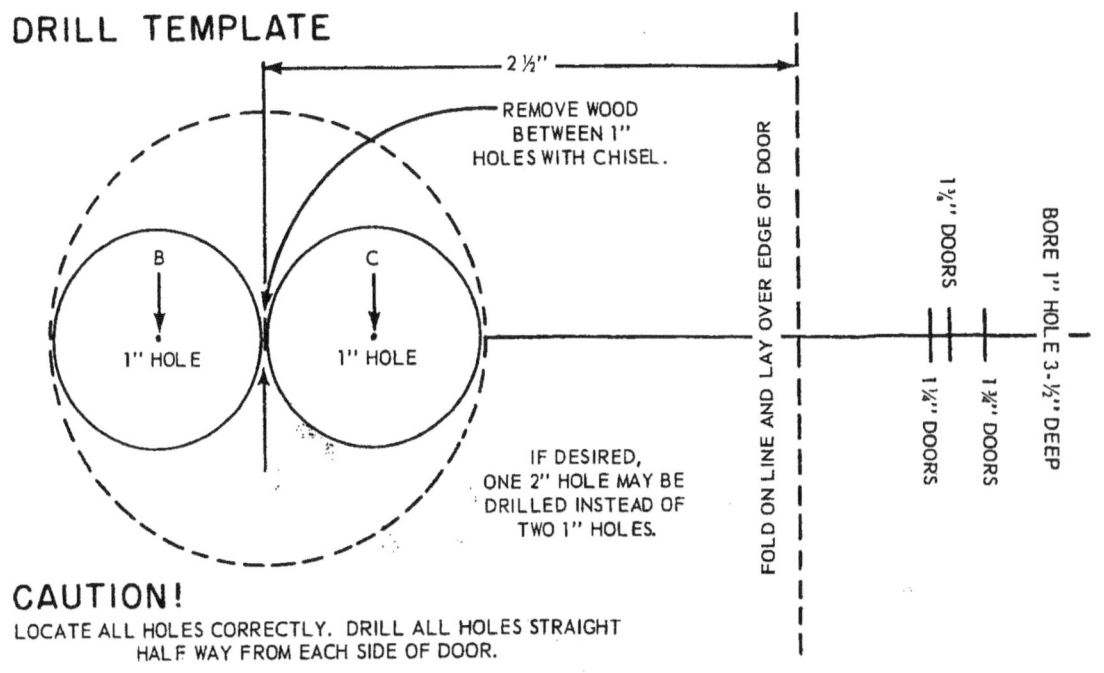

Figure 13-23.—One type of template.

A close-grain wood should be used when the trim is to be painted. However, harder woods free from pitch will provide a better paint surface.

BASEBOARDS

A trim member called a BASEBOARD is usually installed on the line along which the walls join the floors. Baseboard is nailed to the studs with two 6-penny finish nails at each stud crossing. The first step in installing baseboard, therefore, is to locate all the studs in the wall and mark the locations on the floor with light pencil marks.

Baseboard is miter-joined at outside corners and butt-joined at inside corners. Where baseboards cannot be miter-joined or butt-joined at corners, they should be capped. Since the walls at corner baseboard locations may not be perfectly vertical, inside and outside corners should be joined as follows:

To butt-join a piece of baseboard to another piece already in place at an inside corner, set the piece to be joined in position on the floor, bring the end against or near the face of the other piece, and take off the line of the face with a scriber as shown in figure 13-24. Use the same procedure when butting ends of baseboard against the side casings of doors.

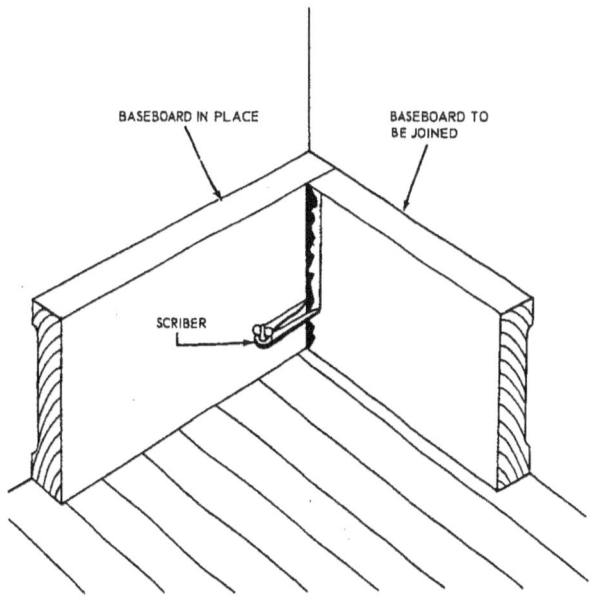

Figure 13-24.—Butt-joining baseboard at an inside corner.

www.ingramcontent.com/pod-product-compliance
Lightning Source LLC
Chambersburg PA
CBHW082208300426
44117CB00016B/2717